The Art of Scottish-American COOKING

The Art of
Scottish-
American
COOKING

KAY SHAW NELSON

PELICAN PUBLISHING COMPANY
GRETNA 2007

Contents

Preface

'Tis great fun and with tremendous pride that Scots don their kilts, tam-o'-shanters, tartans, and tweeds to enjoy the annual Christmas Walk, a joyous celebration of their Scottish heritage, in Alexandria, Virginia on the first weekend in December. *"Ceud Mile Failte"* (a hundred thousand welcomes) rings throughout historic Old Town with a spirited parade of tartan-clad pipe and drum bands, Scottish dancers, reenactment groups, and over 100 clans from near and far with their faithful companions, terriers and hounds, marching behind colorful banners.

Even if there is nary a Campbell, MacDonald, or Morrison in the family tree, it's a thrill to participate in this celebrated community event, traditionally the beginning of the Christmas season in Alexandria. A city long known for its hospitality, playing host to settlers, travelers, and visitors who love its entertainment and festivities, it's a great place and time of year to hoist "a cup o' kindness" and sing the praises of *"guid* Scottish fare."

Founded by Scottish merchants in 1749 when clipper ships brought a thriving tobacco trade to the Potomac River shores, Alexandria is known both as George Washington's hometown and as the Scottish capital of the United States. It was named after a Scotsman, John Alexander, who, in 1670, bought 6,000 acres of land, including what is today the city, for "six thousand pounds of tobacco and cask." Most of the early settlers in the small seaport community were Scots who found the climate and commercial prospects an agreeable change from their austere life and homeland.

Located across the Potomac River from Washington, D.C., Alexandria is one of America's most picturesque cities. It has preserved many of its centuries-old homes, churches, buildings, and taverns, which are still in use and can be reached along treelined cobblestone streets. Scots figured largely in the foundation of the town as well as in its entertainment. Customs from Scotland were retained, and even today Alexandria celebrates those holiday festivities featuring hospitality and the sharing of food and drink. As one proud citizen explains, "Alexandria loves being Scottish," and the city presents a colorful blend of year-round events commemorating its homeland clan, tartan, music, and cookery traditions.

The Christmas Walk began in 1970 and is now sponsored by The Campagna Center, a service association, in conjunction with the City of Alexandria and The St. Andrew's Society. Named after St. Andrew, the patron saint of Scotland, such societies were established in the 18th century to help Scots settle in American locales. Among the first was that of Alexandria, now called The St. Andrew's Society of Washington, D.C., with origins dating back to 1760, a charitable and social organization of men of Scottish birth and ancestry. Its male members like to perpetuate Scottish traditions with good food and drink and the observance of treasured holidays.

In Alexandria and around the country many of the 20 million Americans of Scottish extraction end the December Yule season with the celebration of Hogmanay (Old Year's Night), or New Year's Eve, the liveliest and greatest of all Scottish holidays. An important and merry event when family and friends gather for a ceremonial blessing of the home, it's characterized by cordial exchanges of good wishes and gifts, singing of nostalgic songs, playing of bagpipes, and dancing, as well as enjoying certain traditional dishes. The word is thought to derive from the old French *hoguignane*, meaning the last day of the year.

For years a special Hogmanay observation was held with a public reception at The Carlyle House, built in 1752 by John Carlyle, a city founder and prosperous Scottish merchant. The Georgian stone house is patterned after Craigiehall, in West Lothian, Scotland. A feature of the event was the "first-footing" ceremony performed on the house's terrace by a member of the City of Alexandria's official bagpipe band at midnight. Many of the guests who attended were of Scottish descent and wore their family tartans.

Now Hogmanay is celebrated in many private homes with an annual Old Year's Night Party where guests enjoy the captivating and significant first-footing ceremony. Once the New Year has been announced after the stroke of midnight, everyone waits in anticipation for the arrival of a portentous visitor, the "first foot," whose character and appearance are believed to determine the household's fortune for the coming year. Toasting and greetings are in progress when, in the midst of the gaiety, a loud knock comes on the door. "Someone's first footin' ye," shouts one of the guests, as the celebrating suddenly stops and all eyes turn to see the caller. With luck, it will be a tall, dark-haired man—said to be a sign of good fortune.

The welcome first-footer and later the guests bring handsels (good-luck gifts) symbolizing life, hospitality, and warmth, such as cheese (magic), bread, cake, a lump of coal to place on the fire, red herring (plenty), and always whisky. Then the celebrating and feasting begin, lasting often until dawn. Everyone loves the spirit and sentiment of the observance. The sound of the bagpipes evokes fond memories of past good times and family celebrations.

Food plays a significant role in the New Year's party and each home has a "thumping good supply" of traditional specialties. Among them are haggis (the much-maligned meat-oatmeal pudding often drenched in whisky), smoked fish, cold and hot game dishes, lamb pies, black bun (a rich spicy fruitcake baked in pastry), shortbread in several varieties, gingerbread cakes and loaves, bannocks (breads), oatcakes, scones, spice and fruit cakes, mince pies, creams, and puddings.

The Scottish spirit of conviviality lives on, not only in Alexandria but also throughout the United States and Canada wherever Scots are.

I, like other Scottish Americans, love the lively celebrations called Scottish or Highland Games and Gathering of the Clans, held throughout the country, as well as cherished holiday events that honor ancient spirited traditions with joyous dining and drinking interspersed with exuberant toasts, orations, and melodies. All it takes for a nostalgic get-together is a homey Scottish dish or two and a wee dram to start singing "Annie Laurie," "Comin' thro' the Rye," and "Loch Lomond."

Ever since my childhood in Lebanon, New Hampshire, one of the most attractive towns in New England, I have been fascinated with tales about Scots and Scottish culinary traditions, particularly those centered on the small isle of Cape Breton, just off Nova Scotia's mainland. For this was the beloved homeland of my Scottish parents, Dolina MacAskill and Angus Shaw, and their forebears, the MacLeods and Morrisons, who had settled happily in the inviting coves and impressive highlands to fish, raise sheep, weave, knit, cook, and perpetuate their Scottish heritage.

I was brought up to enjoy the delight and goodness of homemade soups, nutty-flavored oatmeal porridge, delicious scones eaten hot off the griddle, and whole-wheat breads. Over the years, while traveling and living in foreign countries as well as America, I have had the pleasure of enjoying the hospitality of many Scots and Scottish Americans, particularly those in the Washington, D.C., area.

Although Scottish cooking is rarely acknowledged as noteworthy, the descendants of Scots are instinctive, genuine cooks who take great pride in the preparation of food and who added their traditional recipes to the American cuisine, often with remarkable adaptations. This book represents a fascinating repertoire of the varied specialties ranging from wholesome, nutritious dishes to ambrosial sweets and tempting baked symbols of hospitality, especially cakes and buttery shortbread.

The Art of Scottish-American Cooking recognizes and celebrates the rich culinary heritage of Scots who settled in the United States and Canada and their descendants. I hope that it enhances your knowledge of their many contributions, adds variety and interest to your menu, and brightens the dining experiences of everyone who sits at your table.

Acknowledgments

I have a long list of people, publications, and organizations to thank for helping me considerably in my quest for knowledge and recipes to write a Scottish-American tome that is part history book, part travelogue, part cookbook. Above all it is a chronicle to document the importance of the rich culinary heritage of Scots who contributed so much to the dining pleasures of the United States and Canada.

For many years, beginning during my childhood in Lebanon, New Hampshire, where I learned about my Scottish heritage from my parents, and during visits with relatives in other New England locales as well as Cape Breton, Nova Scotia, I have been fascinated with the history, folklore, lifestyles, and cookery of the Scots. I thank them all, especially those kind men and women who spent hours with me in local markets and kitchens, providing marvelous hospitality, friendly conversations, and homemade specialties. From my Scottish kinsmen I learned about the pride in preparing and serving traditional fare.

At the many colorful Highland Games, Gathering of the Clans, holiday celebrations, and informal home events, I met many people who shared their special knowledge and often personal or family recipes with me. It would be impossible to list all the persons who gave me so much. I have also received support from the members of the Clan Shaw Society, MacAskill Sept Society, The Living Legacy of Scotland, The Scottish Literary Forum, and The St. Andrew's Society of Washington, D.C.

I also thank my late husband, Wayne Nelson, for supporting me in my effort to prove that the Scottish Americans do have a fascinating and delectable cuisine that is a pleasure both to cook and to eat. I thank all the friendly Scottish Americans who provided helpful talks and hospitality during my travels and my neighbors and friends who were kind enough to share dishes and meals with me over the years while I tested the recipes. Their comments and useful hints were and are appreciated.

I am indebted to the librarians, culinary historians, and food writers, as well as many publications from which I acquired considerable knowledge. These include *The Scottish Banner*, *The Highlander*, *The Family Tree*, and *Scottish Heritage USA (SHUSA)*, as well as *The Mark of the Scots*, by Duncan A. Bruce, and *How the Scots Invented the Modern World*, by Arthur Herman, among others.

For this book I am especially grateful to my publisher, Milburn Calhoun, and editor, Nina Kooij, for giving me the opportunity to write it and for providing assistance. As always I wish to thank my daughter, Rae, for her continued support and editorial insight while I wrote the book.

Introduction

For 400 years, untold numbers of Scots—Highlanders, Lowlanders, Islanders, and Ulster-Scots, generally known as Scotch-Irish or Scots-Irish—came to America seeking political asylum, religious freedom, adventure, and economic opportunity. Beginning in the spring of 1607 when the first permanent settlement in North America was established on the James River in Tidewater, Virginia, Scottish men and women would play a significant but often unproclaimed role in the development of the United States and Canada.

Scots have a certain mystique about them that is not easily discernible. Their place in our culture is more versatile and important than generally realized. 'Tis a great pleasure to mingle with hundreds of Scottish Americans at the lively, colorful, and meaningful Highland Games and Gathering of the Clans and recognize their lilting speech, exhilarating music of pipes, fiddles, drums, and harp, as well as athletic competitions noted for energy, ingenuity, and talent. As one Scot explains, "We are industrious people, noted for ambition and achievement, being highly motivated and aggressive, but who love to have a good time by perpetuating our culture with characteristic traditions, including favorite dishes and drinks."

In recent years several publications and Scots have heralded many of the far-reaching influences of Scottish immigrants and their descendants on American history. The Scottish Coalition, composed of eight national organizations serving the Scottish-American community principally through research and long-term planning and as a resource for information and guidance, is very active. Most important is the celebration on April 6 of Tartan Day, officially recognized by a U.S. Senate resolution to honor the many contributions Scottish Americans have made to the character and development of the United States. 'Tis a great day with hundreds of thousands of individuals paying homage to the Scots with banquets and festivities. "The Bands Are Marching, The Pipers Are Piping, The Fiddlers Are Fiddling, The Kilts Are Swirling, The Toasts Are Flowing, The Pride Is Showing," claims one salutation.

Scots numbered prominently among the Founding Fathers. Nine of the signatories of the Declaration of Independence were Scottish, and more than thirty men who have served as president of the United States have at least some Scottish ancestry. It was Pres. Woodrow Wilson who declared, "Every line of strength in our history is colored by Scottish blood."

Scottish ingenuity and talent produced some of our country's greatest inventors and scientists. Cyrus McCormick reinvented the reaper and founded the International Harvester Company. Robert Fulton pioneered steamboats and submarines, Samuel F. B. Morse built a functional telegraph and invented the Morse code, and Thomas Edison developed the electric light bulb and phonograph. It was Alexander Graham Bell who invented the telephone and M. G. Marconi, whose mother was Scottish, the radio. Andrew Carnegie made a fortune in the steel business and became known for his philanthropy and the establishment of libraries throughout the English-speaking world.

The beloved poets Archibald MacLeish and Robert Frost were proud of their Scottish heritage, as were the writers Washington Irving, Edgar Allan Poe, and Herman Melville. The Scots also brought their concern for education and from this came a commitment to public schools, colleges, and universities such as Princeton in New Jersey and Carnegie-Mellon in Pittsburgh. William Holmes McGuffey, the son of a Scottish spy for the American forces in the Ohio Indian wars, was one of the great American educators, called "The

Schoolmaster to Our Nation," and best known as the author of McGuffey's Readers. To date they have sold over 125 million copies.

Over the years Scots have had considerable influence on American architecture and art. Robert Mills, an American of Scottish ancestry, designed several buildings in our capital, including the U.S. Treasury and Washington Monument, meant to be the world's largest and most splendid structure. The furniture designer Duncan Phyfe and artists Gilbert Stuart, James McNeill Whistler, Mary Cassatt, and Anna Robertson Moses (Grandma Moses) contributed to the richness of our country's legacy.

Modern-day Americans of Scottish descent include DeWitt and Lila Acheson Wallace, co-founders of *Reader's Digest;* the authors Dale Carnegie, David McCullough, John McPhee, and John Kenneth Galbraith; Earle R. MacAusland, founder and publisher of *Gourmet* magazine; publisher Malcolm Forbes, a gregarious gourmet; and astronauts Neil Armstrong and Alan Bean, who had a MacBean tartan specially woven and took it to the moon on the Apollo 12 flight.

While several publications have documented various Scottish-American achievements that have contributed so much to our history and culture, none before has ever put forth the important and fascinating culinary story, delving into the past and present of a creative and nutritious cookery that evolved in the United States and Canada. For there is a rich, notable Scottish-American food legacy that is best told not only with recipes but also historical data and culinary anecdotes involving personalities and places.

Look at a map of the United States and you'll find any number of towns and cities named Aberdeen, Edinburgh, Glasgow, Scotland, Campbell, Cameron, Douglas, and Crawford, as well as more than a hundred places whose names begin with "Mac" or "Mc."

Immigrants from Scotland who spread out over the countryside and settled primarily in farm areas of the New World brought with them memories and "receipts" for preparing favorite family dishes. For all true Scots, sentimental about their culture and committed to an awareness of their roots, cooking was an attempt to hold on to a sense of identity. They reproduced their traditional dishes as closely as possible with familiar ingredients or strange ones introduced to them by the Indians, who taught them how to use the bounty of their new land. Many of the early food patterns and imaginative dishes and drinks they created centuries ago have lasted through the generations.

Noted for their warm hospitality and sharing of food, Scots belong to Scottish societies and clans and love the conviviality of celebrating traditional holidays. From colonial times Scots not only gathered in their homes for festive meals but they liked to drop into taverns, pubs, or social centers for casual eating and drinking as well as business and political meetings. Several of these "good hostelry" establishments are still in existence, offering fine fare and a historic atmosphere. In Virginia two of the early American dining places are Alexandria's Gadsby's Tavern, built in 1792 and frequented by our early presidents and statesmen, and the Rising Sun Tavern in Fredericksburg.

Just as double-crusted "puddings" are ancestors of American pies, and Auld Man's Milk became the famous eggnog of America when it migrated from Scotland with early settlers, there are many other Scottish recipes that developed into our country's regional favorites. Among these are Southern fried chicken, cured meats, hashes, kale dishes, scones (forerunners to biscuits), griddle cakes, flapjacks, shortbread, butterscotch candy and pie, chess pies, oatmeal porridge and cookies, and ginger cakes, cookies, and bread, to name only a few. Recipes for some of them can be found in early cookbooks such as *The Virginia Housewife Or, Methodical Cook*, 1824, by Mary Randolph, a notable woman of Scottish descent, and *Housekeeping in Old Virginia*, 1879, by Marian Cabell Tyree, the granddaughter of Patrick Henry.

We also have a lengthy Scottish-American legacy of agricultural, culinary, commercial food, and drink achievements, as well as dining establishments founded by remarkable Scots.

Scottish-born Grant Thorburn sold "love apple" or tomato

seeds in New York in 1807 and also promoted tomato culture and cookery. He later established a tomato seed farm. John McIntosh, the youngest son of a Scottish family that immigrated to America about 1776 and settled in New York State, became a farmer in Ontario, Canada, where the apple named for him originated in 1796. A Scots Canadian, David Fife, developed the first hard spring wheat in North America. After John Wallace, a farmer of Scottish ancestry, immigrated to the United States in 1832, his descendants would shape American agricultural policy for a century. Henry A. Wallace would become secretary of agriculture and then vice-president of the United States. In 1846 Mary Johnson of New Jersey invented the hand-cranked ice-cream freezer.

Armour & Co., founded in Chicago by Philip Armour, was by 1923 the largest meat packer in the world. Sir George Grant, a Scottish adventurer, went to Kansas and left behind the first herd of Black Angus cattle in America.

The eccentric clergyman Sylvester Graham, "father of public health in America," invented Graham flour and a classic snack, the Graham Cracker, in 1829, and, later, Granola and Grape-Nuts, to combat malnutrition. An old family tradition holds that the ancestors of Will Keith Kellogg, who founded Kellogg cereals, originated in Scotland. Tillamook Cheddar cheese has been justly famous up and down the West Coast ever since Peter McIntosh brought his secret of making fine Cheddar from Canada to Tillamook County, Oregon. Two families, the Campbells and the Hutchisons of Lookout Mountain, Tennessee, jointly started a milling company and then the Chattanooga Bakery in the early 1900s. The most successful of their products was a sandwich coated with chocolate that we call Moon Pie.

The list goes on with Campbell's Soups, created by Joseph Campbell, who was born in New Jersey to Scottish parents. Angus MacPease from Aberdeen sold the copyright for his wife's version of Scottish pease porridge to Campbell's Soups and it became the nutritious canned split-pea soup. Robertsons, the oldest cafeteria chain in the South, was started by E. H. Robertson as a soda fountain in 1920 in Charleston and is known for its native Low Country fare. J. A. Morrison and G. C. Outlaw opened a cafeteria in Mobile, Alabama, in 1920 and Morrison's Cafeterias went on to become the largest chain in the country. Monterey Jack cheese is named after David Jacks, a Scot who joined the California Gold Rush but got rich making the cheese on his farm in Monterey County. It was Edmund McIlhenny who first made the famous Tabasco sauce with some hot Mexican peppers that he found in his Avery Island, Louisiana, kitchen garden.

Holiday Inns was founded by Charles Kemmons Wilson, an American of Scottish descent, and the Marriott hotel chain was begun in Washington, D.C. by J. Willard Marriott, of partial Scottish descent. McDonald's, the world's most successful restaurant company, was founded by two Irish-American brothers whose forefathers are said to be from Scotland.

Applejack, a brandy, was created in 1698 by William Laird, a Scot who is said to have been seeking a substitute for his native whisky. Laird & Co. of New Jersey, founded by a grandson, Robert, in 1780, still has a virtual monopoly on the manufacture of applejack in the United States.

In 1789 a Scottish frontier Baptist preacher named Elijah Craig of Georgetown, Kentucky, filled some charred barrels with corn and rye whisky he had made. He discovered that the drink changed color, the flavor mellowed, and a tradition was born. The new sour mash was named for Bourbon County, Kentucky, in which it was made.

Dr. James Crow, a physician who emigrated from Edinburgh, Scotland, to Kentucky in 1815, brought science to bourbon production by improving the methods of distillation with his sour-mash process. He is generally given credit for founding the modern bourbon industry; Old Crow Bourbon Whiskey is named for him.

America's most famous whisky is still made in Lynchburg, Tennessee, by relatives of the English-Scotsman Jack Daniel. Other early distillers with Scottish names include Spears, Hamilton, and Stewart.

In his remarkable book, *The Mark of the Scots*, Duncan A. Bruce mentions two Americans who did a great deal "to refine the taste of Americans for fine food" and who have Scottish ancestors. They are the late James Beard, a notable cookbook author who wrote extensively about food and wine, and Craig Claiborne, also a cookbook author, *New York Times* food editor, and critic, whose forefathers came from Aberdeen and settled in various locales of the United States. He wrote about and praised many Scottish dishes, including some he had enjoyed during his childhood in Mississippi.

James Beard was an ardent advocate of American cooking and its "rich and fascinating food heritage." He spoke and often wrote about the culinary traditions of "the many people who have crossed the seas to form our new, still-young nation." Among the American versions of Scottish dishes that he gave recipes for are Scotch Broth, Cullen Skink, Scotch Woodcock, Finnan Haddie, Oatmeal Bread, and Scones.

The late Julia Child, celebrated cook, author, television personality, and OSS veteran, was born of Scottish ancestry as Julia McWilliams. She is remembered for the unadulterated joy she projected on her "French Chef" and other TV programs. In 2003 she received the Presidential Medal of Freedom, our nation's highest civilian honor.

The late M. F. K. Fisher, "Philosopher-Poet of the Stove," once America's foremost gastronomical writer and the author of several notable cookbooks, had Scottish ancestors on her father's side. He gave his family sage advice "gastronomically as well as in several other ways," she wrote. "He wanted us to taste life in the round, with all of our senses as well as our wits to work for us. He considered the art of eating a basic part of the plan."

In *The Art of Scottish-American Cooking* we will explore and enjoy not only sage advice but also backgrounds and recipes for dishes brought over the years from Scotland and created by cooks in the United States and Canada. Hopefully, it will give readers a fascinating and rewarding culinary adventure.

The Art of
Scottish-
American
COOKING

STARTERS

Initially it was nostalgic visits to Pres. Thomas Jefferson's beloved home, Monticello, and Ash-Lawn Highland, an estate once owned by Pres. James Monroe, that drew me to Charlottesville, Virginia, in the foothills of the Blue Ridge Mountains. As it is my custom to take time to enjoy local culinary specialties when I travel, I dined at the Historic Michie Tavern Museum, one of the oldest homesteads in the state. Rich in folklore and history, it was established in the 1700s by Scotsman John Michie, known as "Scotch John," who left an enduring legacy of hospitality while prospering as a businessman.

Born in Scotland and arriving on Virginia's Eastern Shore as an indentured servant with his friend James Watson, John was able to purchase his freedom and have sufficient funds to acquire land in Hanover County by July 1730. Here he toiled as a farmer. A few years later Michie purchased over a thousand acres of land from another Scot, Maj. John Henry, father of the notable orator and patriot, Patrick Henry, and moved his wife, Mary, and three small sons into a modest but commodious dwelling.

Residing along a stagecoach route with few other settlers in the area, the Michie family began welcoming travelers seeking food and shelter. Along with running an inn, or ordinary, "Scotch John" added a tavern that became a popular meeting place where Virginia statesmen and patriots gathered for political talk and to hear the news.

In later years a man by the name of "Booze" began selling fine liquor in bottles that he had designed. Michie Tavern folklore states, "With the outside bar being readily accessible to those in wagons seeking to refresh body and spirit, it became quite common to hear a booming voice demand, 'Aye, lass! Give ta me a bottle of ye booze!'" The word "booze" has been carried down by generations and is often still used to refer to an intoxicant.

In 1927 the historic tavern was moved to its present site, 683 Thomas Jefferson Parkway, where hospitality continues and little has changed in the converted log cabin that offers a historical journey through 18th-century life. The Bill of Fare in the dining room or Ordinary features dishes of the colonial period, including those of Scottish origin, served by waitresses in colonial attire. There is also a gristmill, a general store, and an upstairs museum tracing the history of Virginia's wine production from Jefferson's time to the present.

Tasty and appealing starters, or appetizers, are enjoyed with drinks before a luncheon or dinner or at parties. They are tempting to the eye, pleasing to the palate, and stimulating to the appetite. Some of the varied selection can also be served as snacks, for outdoor meals, and at Scottish Games and Gatherings.

Sassy Pecans from Monticello

The sweet, oily, honey-colored pecan, a native American nut belonging to the hickory family, is a symbol of hospitality and a cherished food whether eaten by itself or used as an ingredient in cookery. A friend gave Thomas Jefferson some wild pecans, which he planted at Monticello. Legend says the president liked them so much that he gave pecan seedlings to George Washington, who grew the trees at his home, Mount Vernon, Virginia, to ensure a constant supply of the nuts, one of his favorite snacks.

2 cups shelled pecan halves
1 tbsp. Worcestershire sauce
1 tbsp. vegetable oil
Salt, to taste

Put pecans in a shallow baking dish. In a small dish combine the Worcestershire sauce and oil. Sprinkle over pecans. Stir to coat all pecans. In a preheated 250-degree oven, bake, stirring occasionally, for 20 minutes. Remove from oven. Sprinkle with salt. Cool. Makes 2 cups.

Peppered Pecans from Louisiana

Ever since the Scotsman Edmund McIlhenny introduced his soon-to-be-famous Tabasco in 1868, tempting recipes have been flavored with the hot sauce. Peppered Pecans, a Louisiana tradition, is one of the classics. This recipe is adapted from *The Tabasco Brand Cookbook.* The pecans may be served as starters or taken on picnics.

3 tbsp. unsalted butter
3 cloves garlic, minced
2½ tsp. Tabasco sauce
½ tsp. salt
3 cups shelled pecan halves

In a small skillet, melt butter over medium-low heat. Add garlic, Tabasco, and salt. Cook 1 minute. Toss pecans with the butter mixture. Spread in a single layer on a baking sheet. In a preheated 250-degree oven, bake, stirring occasionally, for 1 hour, or until pecans are crisp. Makes 3 cups.

Benjamin Harrison's Sausage Rolls

Our twenty-third president, Benjamin Harrison, was a grandson of William Henry Harrison, our ninth president, and both claimed Scottish roots. Benjamin and his wife, Caroline Lavina Scott, entertained frequently at the White House, where they served a variety of nourishing fare for official and family meals. A favorite appetizer was sausage rolls. Mrs. Harrison's recipe for them was printed in an 1890 collection entitled *Statesmen's Dishes*. This is one of my favorite versions of the appetizer, whether hot or cold.

24 link pork sausages
1½ cups all-purpose flour
¾ tsp. salt
½ cup vegetable shortening, cut in small
   pieces
About 4 tbsp. cold water
1 large egg, beaten

In a large skillet, partially cook sausages over medium-high heat to release almost all of the fat. Drain on paper towels; cool.

Into a medium bowl, sift flour and salt. With a pastry blender, cut in shortening until mixture is uniformly crumbly. Gradually add water, enough to make a firm dough. Turn out on a lightly floured surface; roll into a thin rectangle. Cut into 24 strips, each about 2½ x 3 inches. Place a sausage link in center of each strip; roll up, leaving ends of sausage out. Seal pastry edges with a little cold water. Cut 2 small slashes across top of each roll. Brush tops with egg. Place 1 inch apart on a lightly greased baking sheet. In a preheated 425-degree oven, bake for 20 minutes, until crisp. Makes 24.

Scotch Eggs

Following his exploration of Chesapeake Bay, Virginia, in 1631, William Claiborne set up a trading post on Kent Island, the largest of the bay's islands. A colony developed and in 1638 the island became part of Maryland. Claiborne's Landing at the entrance to Stevensville is named after the explorer. One of the best-known American Claiborne descendants is the late notable food writer and cookbook author, Craig Claiborne, who stated that one of his favorite snacks was Scotch Eggs, fried sausage-covered hard-cooked eggs. He described them as being "one of the most basic concepts of cooking." They are favorite pub and picnic fare, enjoyed particularly at Scottish Gatherings, and are also good starters.

6 hard-cooked eggs
All-purpose flour
1 lb. bulk pork sausage
2 tbsp. minced yellow or white onions
2 tbsp. minced fresh parsley
Salt and freshly ground black pepper, to
taste
2 eggs, beaten
About 1 cup fine dry breadcrumbs
Peanut or vegetable oil for deep-frying

Shell eggs; wipe dry with paper towels. Roll each in flour to coat lightly. Set aside. In a large bowl combine sausage, onions, and parsley. Season with salt and pepper; mix thoroughly. Divide mixture into 6 equal portions; flatten into thin rounds. Place 1 floured egg in the center of each round; cover completely with sausage, patting it well. Dip in eggs; coat evenly with breadcrumbs. Place on a large plate. Refrigerate, covered with plastic wrap, up to 12 hours.

To cook, heat 3 inches oil in a deep-fat fryer. Fry eggs, 1 or 2 at a time, turning them, in hot oil (325 degrees) until crisp and golden, about 7 minutes. With a slotted spoon, transfer eggs as they are cooked to drain on paper towels. Serve hot or at room temperature, plain or with mustard. Makes 6 whole or 12 halves.

Stuffed Smoked Salmon Eggs

Scots are very fond of smoked fish, especially salmon, the most luxurious and highly prized. The quality of the North Atlantic fish and the cold smoking technique result in a distinguished flesh. Genuine Scotch smoked salmon is rich and succulent with a distinctly pleasing smoky flavor.

Many Scottish Americans prefer the salmon *au naturel*, without accompaniments. Serve each person a few cold, thin slices (cut diagonally as close to serving time as possible), with a wedge of lemon, a grind or two of black pepper, and thinly sliced buttered or plain brown bread. Or serve thin salmon slices on oatcakes with a garnish of sour cream and chopped fresh dill. These eggs are attractive as well as delicious.

6 hard-cooked eggs, shelled and cut in half
lengthwise
6 oz. smoked salmon, minced
2 tbsp. fresh lemon juice
1 tbsp. grated onion
3 tbsp. sour cream or mayonnaise
Freshly ground black pepper, to taste
Fresh dill sprigs, for garnish

Remove yolks from eggs; mash yolks in a small bowl. Add salmon, lemon juice, onion, and sour cream or mayonnaise. Season with pepper. Mix well. With a small spoon put salmon mixture into egg-white halves, dividing equally and mounding mixture into the shape of an egg. Garnish with dill. Refrigerate, covered, until ready to serve. Makes 12.

Etta MacKay's Salmon Dip

Etta MacKay, a resident of Olney, Maryland, is proud of her thriving business selling imported Scottish smoked salmon and trout that are raised and cured at a family fishery in her hometown of Tobermory, on the island of Mull in Scotland. Silky and succulent, with a unique tang of spices and wood smoke, the salmon blends well with a few ingredients to make this flavorful dip.

8 oz. cream cheese, softened
½ cup sour cream
1 tbsp. fresh lemon juice
¾ cup minced smoked salmon
2 tbsp. snipped fresh chives
Salt and freshly ground white pepper, to
    taste

In a medium bowl combine cheese, sour cream, and lemon juice; blend well. Add salmon and chives. Season with salt and pepper. Blend well. Refrigerate, covered, until ready to serve as a dip for raw vegetables or with oatcakes. Makes about 2 cups.

Ozark Smoked Trout Spread

Many Scottish immigrants moving across the country were captivated by the intense natural beauty of the Ozark Mountains in northwestern Arkansas, where they settled, farmed, and fished. Lyon College, founded in 1872, has celebrated its Scottish connection in many ways, including an Arkansas (Ozark) Scottish Festival. It is one of the premier Scottish events in the south-central United States, held on the last full weekend in April, and its food booths offer a variety of treats from Scotland and the Ozarks. This starter is made with a favorite local food, smoked trout.

1 lb. smoked trout
½ cup sour cream
2 tbsp. fresh lemon juice
3 tbsp. minced chives
⅛ tsp. cayenne pepper
Freshly ground black pepper, to taste

Remove the skin from trout. In a medium bowl mash trout with a fork until smooth (should be about 1½ cups trout). Add sour cream, lemon juice, chives, and peppers. Blend well. Spoon mixture into a 2-cup bowl or crock. Refrigerate, covered with plastic wrap, for 2 to 6 hours. Serve with brownbread triangles or crackers. Makes about 2 cups.

Ingonish Kipper Pâté

Kippers are herrings that have been split, lightly salted, and then smoked. They have a golden-brown color and a delicate smoky taste. Eaten in a variety of ways, canned kippers make a well-flavored spread that can be easily prepared and served in the home or at picnics. I recall enjoying this pâté at a picnic in Ingonish, a summer vacation center and the headquarters and main entrance to the Cape Breton Highlands National Park, 390 square miles of spectacular beauty situated in the northern part of Cape Breton Island, where Scots from the Highlands and Islands settled and continue to live.

2 cans (3¼ oz. each) kipper fillets, drained
and cut up
½ cup (1 stick) unsalted butter, softened and
cut in small pieces
2 tbsp. fresh lemon juice
2 tsp. minced onion
2 tsp. Dijon-style mustard
⅛ tsp. freshly ground black pepper

Puree all ingredients in a blender or food processor. Spoon mixture into an earthenware or glass container. Leave at room temperature 30 minutes. Refrigerate, covered with plastic wrap, for several hours to 2 days. Serve with thin slices of brown bread or toast. Makes 1½ cups.

Dunedin Potted Shrimp

Located midway down Florida's west coast, just a few miles north of Clearwater, the quiet community of Dunedin reflects the rich American and Scottish heritage of its founding fathers. The name is Gaelic for Edinburgh and some of the streets have Scottish names. In early spring when the Highland Games take place, Dunedin brings Scotland to this attractive resort center. Here shrimp is a highly prized food, often made into a paste and put in small pots in the refrigerator until ready to serve.

1 lb. tiny shrimp, shelled, cooked, and
   deveined
1 cup (2 sticks) unsalted butter
1 tbsp. fresh lemon juice
⅛ tsp. freshly grated nutmeg
⅛ tsp. cayenne pepper
6 watercress leaves or parsley sprigs, for
   garnish

Cut shrimp into bits. In a medium saucepan combine 1 stick butter (cubed), lemon juice, nutmeg, and pepper. Cook over medium-low heat until butter melts and is foamy. Stir in shrimp; heat gently until coated with butter. Spoon mixture into 6 small pots, dividing equally.

Put remaining 1 stick butter (cubed) in the saucepan; melt. Pour over shrimp to form a thin layer, dividing equally. At room temperature allow mixture to set. Cover each with plastic wrap. Refrigerate for several hours to 3 days. Leave at room temperature about 1 hour before serving. Garnish each pot with 1 watercress leaf or parsley sprig. Serve with thin slices of brown bread. Serves 6.

Eastern Shore Broiled Oysters

An elegant home and historical landmark, Kerr Place, the finest example of Federal architecture on the Eastern Shore of Virginia, was built in Onancock in 1799 by an immigrant from Scotland, John Shepard Kerr, a prosperous merchant, shipper, and farmer. It is now a museum and the headquarters of the Eastern Shore Historical Society.

Scottish settlers in America became fond of local "sea pearls," or oysters, and dined regularly on them, especially as starters, served plain on the half-shell or, with a little flavoring, grilled or broiled. The recipe below serves 1 person.

4 to 6 fresh oysters
4 to 6 oyster-shell halves
Melted butter
Worcestershire sauce
Minced fresh parsley
Salt and freshly ground black pepper, to
taste

Arrange oysters on half-shells in a shallow baking dish. Mix remaining ingredients and top each oyster with a spoonful. Put oysters under a heated broiler until the edges begin to curl, just a few minutes. Serve with lemon wedges and buttered thin slices of brown bread. Serves 1.

North Carolina Pan-Roasted Oysters

Scottish Americans living in the North Carolina coastal regions around Cape Fear and Wilmington have long enjoyed convivial outdoor gatherings called oyster roasts. Oysters are placed on racks over a fire built over stones in a hole or roasted in a regular outdoor fireplace. Although not as festive, one may have an indoor oyster roast with the following recipe.

2 pints oysters, drained
½ cup (1 stick) unsalted butter, melted
Salt and freshly ground black pepper, to
 taste
8 slices hot buttered toast

Arrange oysters in a buttered shallow baking dish. Pour butter over them. Season with salt and pepper. In a preheated 400-degree oven, bake oysters for about 10 minutes, until the edges curl. Serve at once on toast. Serve with lemon wedges and 1 or 2 dashes of Worcestershire sauce, if desired. Serves 8.

Po' Boy Sandwich

An oyster loaf or sandwich that became popular in New Orleans in the late 19th and early 20th centuries is made with a long, slender loaf of white bread split lengthwise and filled with various foods, including oysters. It was a favorite inexpensive snack called a po' boy, commonly sold by street vendors. According to Scots who lived in the city, this idea was introduced from Edinburgh, Scotland, where oyster loaves were a specialty.

1 small, thin loaf white bread
¼ cup unsalted butter, softened
Fried oysters, drained

Slice bread in half lengthwise and scoop out some of the crumbs from both halves to form a case. Spread butter inside the case. Brown bread halves in a preheated 400-degree oven. Fill bottom half with oysters. Place the top on the loaf and cut into 4 sections. Garnish with sliced pickles, if desired. Serve at once. Serves 4.

Auld Alliance

This whisky-flavored cheese spread is named for Scotland's long years of friendship with France, known as the Auld Alliance. Served as a favorite starter by Scots living in Canada's Quebec City, it is easy to prepare and can be made in several variations. This one includes the addition of walnuts, if desired.

8 oz. cream cheese, softened
2 to 3 tbsp. Scotch whisky
⅓ cup minced walnuts (optional)

Place cheese in a small bowl. Add whisky slowly and blend to make a firm cream. Add walnuts if desired. Pack into a small earthenware pot or a bowl and refrigerate for 3 to 4 hours. Serve with oatcakes, crackers, or toast triangles. Makes about 1 cup.

Ha' Pennies

These crisp Cheddar cheese rounds are a specialty at the annual Christmas Walk, a glorious early-December Scottish celebration in Alexandria, Virginia.

1 cup all-purpose flour
⅛ tsp. cayenne pepper
¼ tsp. salt
½ cup (1 stick) unsalted butter, cool and
diced
2 cups finely shredded Cheddar cheese
4 to 6 tsp. light cream

In a large bowl combine flour, pepper, and salt. With a pastry blender cut in butter until mixture resembles fine crumbs. Stir in cheese. Add cream, 1 tsp. at a time, using enough to make a stiff dough. Gather into a ball. Put on a flat floured surface. With a sharp knife cut into 2 parts. Shape each part into a long roll about 1 inch in diameter. Wrap each roll in plastic wrap. Refrigerate about 2 hours.

Preheat oven to 375 degrees. Put each roll on a flat surface. With a floured sharp knife, cut each roll into ¼-inch slices. Place on ungreased baking sheets, about 1 inch apart. Bake in preheated oven about 12 minutes, until tender and golden. With a spatula transfer to wire racks. Cool. Store in airtight containers. Makes about 4 dozen.

Oregon's Cheese Toasties

An Oregon Cheddar cheese called Tillamook, one of the finest of all Pacific Northwest cheeses, has been justly famous since Peter McIntosh, a Scottish-Canadian and pioneering dairyman, started making it with a surplus of milk in the 1890s. Known for its bright yellow color and uniquely aromatic flavor, Tillamook cheese is standard fare at many parties and is excellent in this specialty.

1 cup grated Tillamook or other Cheddar
  cheese
2 tbsp. mayonnaise
2 tsp. light cream or milk
1 tsp. minced onion
½ tsp. dry mustard
1 tsp. Worcestershire sauce
Dash of cayenne pepper
4 slices white toast
2 slices raw thin bacon, cut into small pieces

In a small bowl combine the cheese, mayonnaise, cream or

milk, onion, mustard, Worcestershire sauce, and pepper; mix well. Remove crusts from toast; spread each toast with some cheese mixture. Cut each toast into 5 strips. Top with bacon pieces. Just before serving, put in a preheated 450-degree oven for 5 minutes. Serve hot. Makes 20.

Hogmanay Herbed Cheese

This is a good starter to serve for New Year's Eve, Hogmanay, a merry gathering of family and friends to celebrate with traditional customs and good fare.

½ lb. (8 oz.) grated Cheddar cheese
Dash of cayenne pepper
3 tbsp. unsalted butter, softened
Pinch of dry mustard
¼ cup Scotch whisky or other liquor
2 tbsp. crushed fresh herbs (parsley, basil,
   thyme)

Combine ingredients in a medium bowl. Beat until smooth. Spoon into a small pot or crock; cover and refrigerate for 24 hours or longer to blend flavors. Leave at room temperature a short time before serving. Serve with oatcakes or crackers. Makes 1¼ cups.

Virginia Campbell's Pickled Mushrooms

Virginia Campbell's Cook Book is a fascinating collection of handwritten recipes that were served in the 1850s at the Campbell House in St. Louis, Missouri. As the wife of Col. Robert Campbell, famous in the annals of frontier adventure for his exploits with explorers, fur traders, and great mountain men of the Wild West, she was a legendary hostess and the Campbells were known for their hospitality.

The Campbell House Foundation interprets and promotes the Campbell House as a museum that educates and encourages an appreciation of 19th-century art and culture through the Robert Campbell family and its role in the development of St. Louis and the American West.

In her cookbook Virginia Campbell has several recipes for mushrooms, including one for pickled mushrooms. This is an adaptation from St. Louis.

1 small white onion, minced
1 bay leaf
½ cup chopped fresh parsley
½ tsp. dried thyme
2 cups white vinegar
2 cups white wine or water
¼ cup vegetable oil
Salt and freshly ground black pepper, to
   taste
1 lb. small fresh mushrooms, cleaned and
   trimmed

In a large saucepan combine onion, bay leaf, parsley, thyme, vinegar, wine or water, and oil. Season with salt and pepper. Bring to a boil over medium-high heat. Add mushrooms. Bring to a boil. Reduce the heat to medium low. Simmer, covered, for 10 minutes, until mushrooms are just tender. Cool and then chill in the liquid for 2 to 6 hours. Drain before serving. Serves 4 to 6.

Soups

Early Scottish settlers in America would have been lost without soups. In their homes the capacious black kettles, filled with hearty soups and hung over a fire in the hearth, provided necessary nourishment and warmth. Later the pots of soup simmered on the black iron stoves. Nothing was easier to make without great expense than soup, and seemingly every edible food went into the pot.

One can say that in soup-making the thriftiness of the Scots was exemplified, for they made simple but nourishing soups with greens, flowers, and roots of wild plants, nuts, beans, seafood, and the meat of wild animals, seasoned with native herbs and other foods. In lean times and while moving across the country, Scottish settlers tossed leftovers into the soup kettle that was always in evidence.

Most of the early housewives prepared broth or hot liquids in which meat, poultry, or fish had been boiled, to drink as snacks or in times of illnesses. Some of these dishes were plain and served with dried breads; some were flavored with vegetables, herbs, or flower petals. Those made with several greens and herbs in the spring were favored as tonics.

The Scots learned from the Indians how to make a concentrated essence of soup, the bouillon cube of the time, which was most convenient to use whether in the home, at sea, or while traveling. The inventive cooks created their versions of Portable Soup, Soup-In-His-Pocket, or Pocket Soup, as it was called, made with a complicated recipe requiring the boiling of large quantities of veal or beef stock (and pigs' trotters), which was reduced, pressed, cut in flat pieces, and dried. If kept in a dry place, the soup would last for years. Scots going from the East Coast moving westward evidently found it very effective and nourishing. One Virginia traveler wrote, "If you should faint with fasting or fatigue, let a small piece of this glue melt in your mouth and you will find yourself surprisingly refreshed."

In the northern New England locales, soups were commonly frozen in large wide-mouthed kettles and hung in cold back pantries to be used during winter months. Chunks could be easily chopped off and heated with the required amount of water.

Scots prepared many economical soups that had names such as Old-Fashioned Scrap Soup, Poor Man's Soup, Cheap Soup, Soup Maigre, and Common Soup. Yet during the 19th and early 20th centuries, eras of lavish dining, Scots living in such cities as Philadelphia, Boston, Charleston, Williamsburg, and Atlanta relished a great variety of intricate soups. Cooks had stockpots and soup kettles in which they made stocks, consommés, bisques, and rich cream soups. Just about every household had a handsome soup tureen from which soups were proudly ladled into wide plates or two-handled bowls. Soup played a significant role in the daily menu, and robust soups were ever available for breakfasts, midday dinners, and suppers.

When high-quality convenience foods became readily available and homemakers could buy canned, dehydrated, and frozen soups, as well as bouillon cubes in abundance, the interest in making soups from scratch lessened somewhat. An important milestone in the commercial preparation of canned soups was the introduction of Campbell's condensed products. The business that became the Campbell Soup Company began in 1869. In that year Joseph Campbell, born in 1817 in Bridgeton, New Jersey, to James and Hannah Campbell, two Scottish-American Presbyterians, and Abram A. Anderson established a canning and preserving plant at Camden, New Jersey. The young firm soon gained a reputation for its fine products, including vegetables, preserves, salad dressings, and ketchup. In 1892 the business was incorporated under the name Joseph Campbell Preserve Company (later shortened to Joseph Campbell Company). Over the years various new products were added to the line.

The turning point in Campbell's history was in 1897 when a young Campbell chemist named Dr. John T. Dorrance developed condensed soup. He conceived the idea of double-strength concentrate with just one-half of the liquid content, the remaining liquid to be added by the cook. The famous red-and-white cans, today a familiar sight on grocery-store shelves, became household staples. *Helps for the Hostess*, published by the Joseph Campbell Company in 1916, advised the women of the day on how to give "a successful formal dinner" and an "informal dinner with one maid" by serving condensed soups. By 1922 Campbell had become the world's best-known name in soups and "cooking with Campbell's" has long been a favorite byword among American homemakers, who use their numerous cookbooks to make all kinds of specialties.

The ready-made soups, good when heated individually, also were combined with other canned soups to produce interesting variations, or enhanced with additional seasonings or solid foods. Many favorite "soup mates" have been suggested by the manufacturers or created by cooks at home.

Soup-making has long been one of the special skills of the Scottish-American housewife, who, despite the popularity of canned soups, continued to prepare the marvelous repertoire of national favorites. The names of the Scottish soups were as imaginative as their ingredients. *Powsowdie* is sheep's-head broth; *Skink*, a vegetable-beef soup; *Feather Fowlie*, a creamy chicken soup; *Nettle Kail*, a cockerel, nettle, and oat soup; and *Bawd Bree*, a hare soup.

Close to the hearts of all of us are savory soups that can be enjoyed hot or cold on any occasion, and at any time of day. Soup is a never-fail gastronomic winner. Reliable as an old and trusted friend, it also has the appeal and sparkle of a new acquaintance.

It was a notable Scot, H. V. Morton, who wrote a marvelous accolade to two special Scottish soups. He could "live on Scotch broth and cocky-leekie for ever," he stated. "These supreme soups, the absolute monarchs of the stock-pot, are unparalleled elsewhere in the world. They are the food of the Gods."

Scotch Broth

The most traditional of all Scottish soups is one called Barley Broth or Scotch Broth, a treasured family dish made with mutton or lamb, barley, and vegetables. In his *American Cookery*, James Beard wrote, "The Scot is anonymous who introduced this dish to American cookery, but it has remained a favorite for more than a century. As is true of many soups, its contents vary a good deal." 'Tis a good winter supper dish.

2 lb. neck or breast of lamb, cut up
2 qt. water
Salt, to taste
½ cup pearl barley
Freshly ground black pepper, to taste
1 cup peeled, diced carrots
1 cup sliced yellow or white onions
1 medium turnip, peeled and diced
3 tbsp. chopped fresh parsley

Put lamb into a large pot. Add water; season with salt. Bring to a boil over medium-high heat. Skim off any scum from the top. Add barley. Season with pepper. Reduce the heat to medium low. Cook slowly, covered, for 2 hours. Take off the stove. With tongs, remove meat and cool. Cut meat from bones. Trim any fat from meat. Return meat to the pot. Discard bones and fat. Add carrots, onions, and turnip. Bring to a boil over medium-high heat. Lower the heat to medium low. Cook slowly, covered, for 30 minutes, or until ingredients are cooked. Correct the seasoning. Stir in parsley. Serves 6.

Cock-a-Leekie

This celebrated, imaginative, and nourishing Scottish chicken and leek soup is a beloved family and company dish that is known around the world and immortalized in literature. "Come, my lords and lieges, let us all to dinner, for the cocky-leekie is a-cooling," wrote Sir Walter Scott in *The Fortunes of Nigel*. And a favorite accolade goes: "Lang may ye live, an' long enjoy/Ilk blessin' life can gie,/Health, wealth, content and pleasure,/An cock-a-leekie."

Some Scots trace the soup's creation to Edinburgh during the days of the Auld Alliance. Most old recipes called for a cock, presumably an old bird, preferably plump. Others say that the name derives from the time when cockfighting was a popular sport and the defeated bird ended up in the soup pot, with leeks added to give more flavor.

Scottish Americans serve this soup at family and clan gatherings. One cook explained, "We sometimes add halved and pitted prunes to 'sweeten' the soup, as they once did in Scotland. They provide an interesting topic for conversation." For those who wish to have a one-dish meal, potatoes can be added to the soup.

1 stewing chicken, about 5 lb.
5 qt. water
12 leeks, white parts and 2 inches green
    stems, washed and cut into ¼-inch lengths
4 parsley sprigs
1 bay leaf
½ tsp. dried thyme
1 tbsp. salt
½ tsp. freshly ground black pepper
½ cup pearl barley
8 dried prunes, halved (optional)
¼ cup chopped fresh parsley

Put chicken and water into a large pot. Bring to a boil over medium-high heat. Skim the top. Add leeks, parsley sprigs, bay leaf, thyme, salt, and pepper. Reduce the heat to medium low. Cook slowly, partially covered, for about $2^1/_2$ hours, until chicken is tender. Add barley 1 hour before serving. About $^1/_2$ hour before serving, add prunes, if desired. After the full cooking time, remove chicken to a platter. When cool enough to handle, remove chicken meat, discarding skin and bones; cut meat into bite-size pieces. Remove and discard parsley and bay leaf from the liquid. Skim. Return chicken to the kettle. Put the soup back on the stove long enough to heat through. Serve garnished with chopped parsley. Serves 8 to 10.

Mulligatawny

This hearty well-seasoned chicken soup was first eaten by Scottish soldiers serving in India, and it arrived in the American South by way of descendants of these fighting men. The name is derived from an Indian word meaning "pepper water," and the soup was sometimes called "curry soup." This version always wins applause.

1 frying chicken, about 3 lb., cut up
1 medium onion stuck with 4 cloves
2 medium carrots, peeled and thickly sliced
1 rib celery, thickly sliced
6 cups chicken broth
Salt and freshly ground black pepper, to
   taste
¼ cup (½ stick) unsalted butter
1 large yellow onion, thinly sliced
2 tbsp. turmeric powder
1 tsp. ground coriander
1 tsp. cayenne pepper
1 clove garlic, crushed
⅓ cup all-purpose flour
1½ cups grated coconut, preferably
   unsweetened
About 2 cups hot cooked rice
1 large lemon, sliced

Put chicken into a large kettle. Add onion with cloves, carrots, celery, and chicken broth. Season with salt and pepper. Bring to a boil over medium-high heat. Reduce the heat to medium low. Cook slowly, covered, for about 30 minutes, until the chicken is tender. With tongs take out the chicken pieces. Cool. Remove meat from the bones; cut meat into bite-size pieces, discarding the skin and bones. Strain and reserve the broth.

In a large kettle melt butter over medium-low heat. Add

onion slices; sauté until tender, about 3 minutes. Add turmeric powder, coriander, cayenne pepper, and garlic. Cook slowly for 1 minute. Stir in flour; cook for 1 or 2 minutes. Gradually add the strained broth and then coconut. Cook slowly, stirring often, for 10 minutes. Add cooked chicken pieces and leave on the stove long enough to heat through. Serve in wide soup bowls. Put rice in a bowl and lemon slices on a plate. Pass them to each person to be added to the soup as garnishes. Serves 6.

Campbell's Mock Lobster Soup

Two of my friends named Campbell who are not fond of cooking soups serve this innovative shortcut soup as a first course for luncheon or dinner when entertaining. They jokingly refer to it as a family recipe rather than telling guests that it is a "soup mate," created and promoted by Campbell's Soups.

The Campbell Highland Games & Celtic Festival are held each June in Campbell, California.

1 can (10½ oz.) condensed pea soup
1 can (10¾ oz.) condensed tomato soup
2 soup cans light cream or milk
3 tbsp. dry sherry
1 tsp. Worcestershire sauce
Dash of Tabasco sauce
Salt and freshly ground black pepper, to
    taste

Combine ingredients in a blender or food processor. Whirl or process to blend. Serve chilled or hot. Serves 6.

Down-East Split-Pea Soup

The dried or split pea, both yellow (made from field peas) and green (made from green peas), has been a staple in the Scottish diet for generations. Primarily it was used to make nourishing soups flavored with vegetables, herbs, and sometimes a meaty ham bone.

According to Scottish lore, it was Angus MacPease from Aberdeen, Scotland, who combined green peas with grain and marketed the product as a staple food. When his wife, Dolly, developed a recipe that had a liquid consistency when hot, and resembled a porridge when cold, their son called the mixture pease porridge and penned a jingle. It went: "Pease porridge hot/In your breakfast bowl. Start your day, the porridge way/E're your health will grow." The more contemporary verse goes: "Pease porridge hot, pease porridge cold, pease porridge in the pot, nine days old."

Later, after Angus immigrated with his family to America, he sold the copyright for his wife's version of Scottish pease porridge to Campbell Soups, and the canned version of green split-pea soup became an American staple.

This recipe is from the New England region known as Down East, especially Maine, where the thick puree makes a delicious supper dish when served with sliced bacon on warm cornbread.

1 lb. (2 cups) dried yellow split peas,
  washed and picked over
8 cups water
½ lb. Canadian bacon
2 large yellow onions, minced
2 large ribs celery, thinly sliced
Salt and freshly ground black pepper, to
  taste

Combine peas and water in a large pot. Bring to a boil over medium-high heat. Boil, uncovered, for 2 minutes Remove from the heat. Let stand, covered, for 1 hour. Add bacon, onions, and celery. Bring to a boil. Lower the heat to medium low. Cook slowly, covered, for about 2 hours, until peas are tender and mixture is thick. Season with salt and pepper.

Remove bacon; cut into thin slices. Serve bacon on slices of warm cornbread or corn sticks with the soup, if desired. Serves 6.

Daniel Webster's Fish Chowder

Daniel Webster, the notable New Hampshire statesman and American secretary of state of Scottish descent, relished fish chowder, and in an 1842 recipe for it, which bears his name, he recommended it "for a large fishing party." You begin with "a cod of ten pounds, well cleaned, leaving on the skin," it stipulates. "Cut into pieces one and a half pounds thick, preserving the head whole." This fish was arranged in layers with sliced salt pork and potatoes, sprinkled with salt and pepper, and boiled in water, to which milk and crackers were later added.

This recipe for fish chowder is from a Scottish-American friend who is from New Hampshire.

1 lb. cod or haddock fillets
¼ cup diced salt pork
1 large yellow onion, sliced
2 cups boiling water
2 cups peeled, diced potatoes
2 cups hot light cream or milk
Salt and freshly ground black pepper, to
    taste
4 unsalted soda crackers, split in halves

Cut fish fillets into 1-inch pieces. In a large saucepan over medium-high heat, fry salt pork to release all the fat and until crisp. Add onion slices; sauté until tender, 4 minutes. Pour in water; add potatoes. Reduce the heat to medium low. Cook slowly, covered, for about 10 minutes, until potatoes are just tender. Add fish. Continue cooking slowly, about 8 minutes longer, until fish flakes easily and potatoes are tender. Add cream or milk. Season with salt and pepper. Serve in 4 soup bowls over halved crackers. Serves 4.

Northwestern Salmon Bisque

'Tis true that many a Scottish cook likes to brag about a favorite dish. Once a lass named Kate ladled a bowl of her salmon soup for my evening meal and told me, "This is provided in Heaven for good Scots."

Some of the best salmon soups, including rich and flavorful bisques, are made in Oregon and Washington, where the fish is highly prized for its rich flavor and fine texture. It is also a good source of calcium, iodine, and phosphorous.

1 small onion, minced
2 tbsp. unsalted butter
2 tbsp. all-purpose flour
1 can (l lb.) tomatoes, undrained and
    chopped
¼ tsp. dried rosemary or thyme
Salt and freshly ground black pepper, to
    taste
1 can (l lb.) red or pink salmon, skin and
    bones removed
3 cups light cream or milk, scalded
¼ cup dry sherry

In a large saucepan over medium-low heat, sauté onion in

butter until tender, 3 minutes. Add flour and cook, stirring, for 2 minutes. Add tomatoes and rosemary or thyme. Season with salt and pepper. Cook slowly, stirring frequently, for 10 minutes. Add salmon and its liquid, then cream or milk. Reduce heat to low and allow bisque to blend flavors for 5 minutes. Remove from the heat; stir in sherry. Serves 6 to 8.

Outer Banks Clam Chowder

The Scots who live on North Carolina's eastern coast or Outer Banks, a chain of narrow, sandy islands spanning many miles, popular for its sand beaches, picturesque villages, and sport and commercial fishing, prepare many inviting soup-stews with various kinds of fish and shellfish. Some have curious names like Muddle or Pine Bark Stew, named for the bark used to kindle the open fire over which it is cooked. This easy-to-prepare chowder can be made with clams in the shell or minced clams and served as a snack or first course.

2 cans (6½ oz. each) minced clams
4 thin slices bacon
1 large yellow onion, minced
2 cups peeled, diced waxy potatoes
2 tbsp. Worcestershire sauce
Salt and freshly ground black pepper, to
  taste

Strain clams; reserve liquid and add enough water to make 2 cups. Set aside. In a large saucepan over medium-high heat, fry bacon to render the fat and until crisp. Add onion; sauté until tender, 4 minutes. Add potatoes and clam liquid with water. Bring to a boil. Reduce the heat to medium low. Cook slowly, covered, until potatoes are tender, about 12 minutes. Add clams and Worcestershire sauce. Season with salt and pepper. Leave on the stove long enough to heat through and blend flavors. Serves 4.

Pikes Peak Partan Bree

A rich cream of crab soup that originated with fishermen in the Western Scottish Islands is a great favorite of many Scots who enjoy seafood, including the members of the Scottish Society of the Pikes Peak, Colorado, region. They are fond of soup-supper potlucks on chilly meeting nights, when this soup is often a featured dish. *Partan* is Gaelic for crab and *bree* means broth.

2 cups chicken broth
¼ cup long-grain rice
1 tbsp. unsalted butter
1 cup flaked, cleaned fresh crabmeat
1 flat anchovy fillet, minced, or 1 tsp.
  anchovy paste
2 cups hot milk
½ cup heavy cream
Ground white pepper, to taste
2 tbsp. chopped fresh parsley or watercress,
  for garnish

In a large saucepan, combine chicken broth, rice, and butter. Bring to a boil over medium-high heat. Reduce the heat to medium low. Cook slowly, covered, for about 20 minutes, until rice is tender. Add ½ cup crabmeat and anchovy or paste. Puree in a food processor or food mill. Return to the rinsed saucepan. Reheat over low heat. Add milk, cream, and remaining crabmeat. Season with pepper. Cook slowly for 1 or 2 minutes. Serve garnished with parsley or watercress. Serves 4.

Jerusalem Artichoke Soup

The Jerusalem artichoke, a light-brown gnarled root and economical, easy-to-grow native American vegetable, became a favorite of Scottish settlers, who learned how to cook it from the Indians, who called it "sun root." Curiously, the knobby vegetable is not related to the globe artichoke and has nothing to do with the city of Jerusalem. A tuber that is a member of the sunflower family, it has an appealing white and crisp flesh with a pronounced sweetish flavor and is cooked like the potato.

The vegetables are often marketed as "sun chokes."

¼ cup (½ stick) unsalted butter
1 cup minced onions
½ lb. Jerusalem artichokes (sun chokes),
    peeled and cubed
4 cups chicken broth
½ tsp. celery seed
1 bay leaf
Salt and freshly ground black pepper, to
    taste
2½ cups light cream
¼ cup grated yellow cheese

In a large saucepan, melt butter over medium-high heat. Add onions; sauté until tender, 4 minutes. Add artichoke cubes, chicken broth, celery seed, and bay leaf. Season with salt and pepper. Bring to a boil. Reduce heat to medium low. Cook slowly, covered, for about 25 minutes, until artichokes are tender. Remove from the heat. Remove and discard bay leaf. Puree mixture in a blender or food processor. Return mixture to the rinsed saucepan. Reheat. Add cream and cheese. Heat slowly for 5 minutes, until cheese is melted. Serve garnished with croutons, if desired. Serves 6 to 8.

West Virginia Watercress Soup

Get-togethers called "Soups," given by church groups and civic organizations as socials and to raise money, were once enjoyed by Scottish Americans living in West Virginia. Members contributed the various ingredients and the soups were cooked in gigantic kettles and served with homemade breads, followed by ice cream and cake for dessert.

Although this custom is no longer common, it is fondly remembered and soup remains a perennial favorite throughout the state. In the spring, Scottish cooks prepare nourishing soups made with a variety of fresh greens, especially watercress, a tangy aromatic herb rich in calcium and vitamin C. There is even an old belief that watercress sharpens the memory.

2 bunches watercress
1 cup boiling, salted water
4 tbsp. unsalted butter
1 small onion, minced
4 tbsp. all-purpose flour
Freshly ground black pepper, to taste
3 cups light cream or milk

Carefully wash watercress in cold water; remove any stems. Combine leaves with boiling water in a large saucepan over medium-high heat. Cook, covered, until tender, about 10 minutes. Puree and set aside. Rinse the saucepan. Add butter; melt over medium-low heat. Add onion; cook until tender, about 2 minutes. Mix in flour. Season with salt and pepper. Cook for 1 minute. Gradually add cream or milk. Cook slowly a few minutes, until thickened and smooth. Add watercress. Leave on the stove just long enough to heat through. Serves 4.

Connecticut Cream of Onion Soup

This old-fashioned soup has long been savored by Scottish Americans in Connecticut, the nutmeg state, known since colonial times for its onions, one of the first farm products to become a quick-money crop.

Scots in Connecticut celebrate their heritage and traditions with yearly Round Hill Highland Games, which claim to have the longest record of consecutive gatherings anywhere in America. Their first meeting in 1923 was a picnic for Scottish immigrants at the estate of R. Calhoun in Stamford, where the Round Hill Games were held for several years. One woman explained, "We don't serve onion soup at the Games but we enjoy it for other Scottish get-togethers. It's one of our traditional dishes."

2 medium yellow onions, thinly sliced
3 tbsp. unsalted butter
2 cups chicken broth or water
2 tbsp. all-purpose flour
⅛ tsp. grated nutmeg
Salt and freshly ground black pepper, to
   taste
2 cups hot light cream

In a large saucepan, sauté onions in butter over medium-low heat until tender, 4 minutes. Add broth or water. Cook slowly, covered, for 15 minutes. In a small dish, mix some of the hot liquid with the flour; blend well. Stir into the saucepan, mixing well with a whisk. Add nutmeg. Season with salt and pepper. Cook slowly, stirring, for 5 minutes. Add cream. Leave on low heat for 1 to 2 minutes. Serve with croutons, if desired. Serves 4.

Texas Oatmeal Soup

Scots have long prepared various kinds of soups with oats or oatmeal. A basic crowdie, or oatmeal soup, is made with stock, oatmeal, and sometimes flavorings and served with potatoes. Oatmeal is also added to traditional kale soup.

Scottish Americans living in Texas enjoy attending the Oatmeal Festival, held every Labor Day weekend in a small town called Oatmeal in Burnet County, about forty miles northwest of Austin.

This simple, creamy, onion-flavored soup that is a typical economical dish can be made also with buttermilk instead of the milk.

1 medium yellow onion, minced
2 tbsp. unsalted butter
¼ cup old-fashioned rolled oats
2 cups chicken broth
Salt and freshly ground black pepper, to
    taste
2 cups light cream or milk
3 tbsp. chopped fresh parsley, for garnish

In a large saucepan, sauté onion in butter over medium-low heat for 2 minutes. Add oats; cook 1 to 2 minutes. Add chicken broth; bring to a boil over medium-high heat. Season with salt and pepper. Reduce the heat to medium low. Cook slowly, covered, for 30 minutes. Strain the mixture. Return liquid to the pan. Add cream or milk. Heat for 2 to 3 minutes. Serve garnished with parsley. Serves 4.

Egg and Cheese Dishes

From the time that Scottish immigrants arrived in America and chickens and cows became staple farm animals, eggs and cheese have been basic foodstuffs and dishes made with them, either separately or combined, are varied and still popular.

In practically all the regions of our country there are local egg and cheese casseroles, puddings, omelets, soufflés, and other rich and creamy dishes that are easy to prepare, economical, and a boon to any cook looking for attractive and nutritious dishes.

One of nature's almost perfect foods, the egg is highly valued for the amount and high quality of protein it contains. Eggs are important to all aspects of cookery, as they are used in every type of dish. Treasured for its versatility, the egg is a fundamental ingredient of many Scottish specialties, including the basic methods of cooking (soft or hard cooked, baked, fried, poached, or scrambled), prepared and seasoned according to traditional preferences, as well as innovative creations with amusing names such as Scotch Woodcock and rarebit.

Eggs have always played an important role in the Scottish diet, and the heart of a traditional breakfast has long been fried eggs with bacon and toast, sometimes garnished with fried mushrooms and grilled tomatoes. A morning repast might include three or four egg dishes, anything from shirred or baked eggs to those fried or scrambled. One Scottish lady recalls family-favorite egg dishes that included the beloved flaked kippers, or kippered herring, as well as Finnan Haddie. Another nostalgic dish was a bread and crowdie (cottage cheese) omelet.

Early self-reliant, frugal, and hardworking Scottish-American farmers who kept several cows and had a surplus of milk turned to making cheeses similar to those that they had known in their homeland and that could be kept or transported and sold. Most of the cheeses were varieties of the kind we call Cheddar but were made in several different versions. By the late 1800s, cheese-making had developed in several American regions, and a few notable Scots contributed to the origins of some excellent cheeses.

One of the earliest states that became known for making cow's-milk cheeses was Vermont, where nearly every town had one or more cheese-making operations, many of them family owned and producing a type of Cheddar that was sharp, almost white, and well cured.

Today the historic Plymouth Cheese Factory in Plymouth Notch, situated in a beautiful area of central Vermont near Woodstock, where many Scots settled, continues with its commercial and storied past. It is steeped in tradition, established in 1890 by Col. John Coolidge, father of our 30th president, Calvin Coolidge, who had a Scottish ancestry and was born and took the oath of office in Plymouth. The factory produces special versions of a raw-milk cheese that is plain (mild, medium, extra-sharp) or in a variety of flavors with a high moisture content that is good for eating and for cooking. Visitors may tour the factory, purchase the cheese, and visit historic buildings, many of which the Coolidge family either built or occupied.

As previously mentioned, a cheese that ranks with the finest Cheddars made anywhere in America is Tillamook, a word that Native Americans of the Pacific Northwest used to describe "a land of many waters," for the seven mountain rivers that run through it. In the heart of Oregon's most famous cheese settlement is Tillamook County Creamery Association, a farmer-owned cooperative, noted for its premium white and yellow Cheddars. It continues the tradition of producing top-quality cheese started over a century ago by a pioneering dairyman, the canny Scottish Canadian named Peter McIntosh. In 1894 his cheese became an immediate success. Over time the business added several more products noted for their hearty flavor and good texture. One notable specialty is the extra-sharp Vintage White Cheddar.

It was a Scotsman named David Jacks, born in Crieff, who in 1849 arrived in California to seek his fortune and ended up owning more land in Monterey County than anyone else. With fourteen dairy ranches among his possessions, the landowner, using old mission recipes and cow's milk, began making in the 1890s a soft, white, smooth cheese with an acid tang. Initially marketed as Jacks' cheese, the original American product was soon simply called Monterey Jack by customers, and the name stuck. Chopped jalapeño peppers are often added to the curd during the cheese-making process. There's also a hard, pale yellow Dry Jack, which has a sharp, nutty flavor and is ideal for eating and grating.

Here is a representative collection of the egg and cheese dishes that Scottish Americans have enjoyed over the years. These recipes are especially good for everyday breakfasts and informal meals.

Scotch Woodcock

If you want to start a congenial discussion about the mystique of this traditional Scottish specialty, a glorified version of scrambled eggs, ask any friendly dining companion about its origin. How it got its name remains unknown, and some people regard it as some kind of a Scottish joke. One explanation is that a hunter came home with his bags empty and because there was no woodcock, a game bird having a long bill and short legs, to serve the guests, he scrambled some eggs. He or somebody else added the anchovies. Once served as a savory at the end of the meal or as an evening snack, it is enjoyed by most Scots today for breakfast or lunch.

This recipe is one of several variations.

8 egg yolks
1 cup heavy cream
Freshly ground black pepper, to taste
3 tbsp. unsalted butter
4 slices hot buttered toast
4 tsp. anchovy paste
8 flat anchovy fillets, drained
2 tsp. chopped fresh parsley

In a medium bowl, whisk yolks and cream. Season with pepper.

In a medium skillet, melt butter over medium-low heat. Pour in egg mixture. Cook, stirring constantly with a wooden spoon, until soft and creamy. Quickly spread each slice of toast with 1 tsp. anchovy paste. Arrange on individual plates. Spoon an equal portion of scrambled eggs over toast. Crisscross 2 anchovy fillets over each portion. Sprinkle each with ½ tsp. parsley. Serve at once. Serves 4.

Drappit Eggs

Some old-time Scots in America still use the colorful term "drappit eggs" for poached eggs. This specialty is easy to prepare and serve for a company breakfast.

4 slices hot buttered toast
4 tsp. ham or kipper pâté
4 hot poached eggs, drained
Salt and freshly ground black pepper, to
   taste
2 tsp. chopped fresh parsley

Spread each slice of toast with pâté. Arrange on individual plates. Top each with a poached egg. Sprinkle with salt, pepper, and parsley. Serve at once with bacon or sausage patties. Serves 4.

Pickled Eggs

For an evening clan meeting serve these pickled eggs with slices of cold cooked ham, turkey, or chicken or use as a garnish for salads. In Scotland the eggs are commonly served as what is called pub fare.

1½ cups cider vinegar
1½ tbsp. granulated sugar
6 whole cloves
2 tsp. mustard seed
½ tsp. salt
Freshly ground black pepper, to taste
6 hard-cooked eggs, shelled

In a medium saucepan, combine vinegar, sugar, cloves,

mustard seed, salt, and pepper over medium-high heat. Bring to a boil; boil for 5 minutes; strain. Put eggs in a jar or plastic container. Cover with the hot strained liquid. Refrigerate, covered, for 2 to 4 days. Drain before serving. Serves 6.

Egg Cutlets

In my hometown of Lebanon, New Hampshire, thrifty Scottish-American cooks created this inexpensive egg specialty to serve their family for supper.

3 tbsp. unsalted butter
4 tbsp. all-purpose flour
Salt and freshly ground black pepper, to
**   taste**
1 cup milk
½ tsp. dry mustard
¼ tsp. paprika
2 tbsp. minced fresh parsley
4 hard-cooked eggs, shelled and chopped
2 eggs, beaten
About 1½ cups dry breadcrumbs
About 3 tbsp. vegetable oil

In a medium saucepan, melt butter over medium-high heat. Stir in flour. Cook, stirring, until smooth, about 1 minute. Season with salt and pepper. Gradually add milk. Cook, stirring, until thickened and smooth. Add mustard, paprika, parsley, and chopped eggs. Mix well. Remove from the heat. Cool and then chill. Shape into cutlets or patties (several small ones per person). When ready to cook, dip each one in beaten egg and then in breadcrumbs. In a large skillet, heat oil over medium-high heat. Add the cutlets. Fry about 4 minutes on one side, and then turn once and fry about 4 minutes on the other side, until heated through and golden on each side. Serves 4 to 6.

Bacon and Egg Cups

This is an attractive dish to serve for a Scottish High Tea or supper.

12 thin slices bacon, partially cooked
12 eggs
Salt and freshly ground black pepper, to
  taste
2 tbsp. chopped fresh dill or parsley
12 rounds hot buttered toast

Coil 1 slice bacon around the inside of a custard or muffin cup. Break 1 egg inside each bacon ring. Sprinkle with salt, pepper, and dill or parsley. In a preheated 375-degree oven, bake for about 12 minutes, until bacon is cooked and eggs are set. Carefully remove from cups and serve on toast rounds. Serves 12.

Note: Each cup may also be served on a scone slice or oatcake.

Cheese Scramble

In many rural Scottish-American homes, a favorite supper dish was a version of scrambled eggs called a scramble that included cheese but sometimes also diced cooked potatoes, ham, or smoked fish.

8 eggs, room temperature
⅓ cup light cream or milk
Salt and freshly ground black pepper, to
**   taste**
½ cup grated Cheddar cheese
⅓ cup unsalted butter

Break eggs into a medium bowl. Add cream or milk. Season with salt and pepper. Stir in cheese. Mix with a fork or wire whisk to combine thoroughly if a uniform color is desired, or mix slightly if streaks of white and yellow are desired. In a medium skillet over medium high, melt butter. Pour in the egg mixture all at once. Reduce heat to medium low and, as soon as mixture begins to set, stir, scraping sides and bottom. Cook until eggs are thickened but still moist and shiny, about 5 minutes. Serve plain or over hot buttered toast or oatcakes. Serves 4.

Deviled Eggs

This old-time favorite, hard-cooked eggs stuffed with a mixture of yolks and hot seasonings and called deviled or "devilled," is popular at picnics and may be served at Scottish Games and Gatherings.

6 hard-cooked eggs, shelled
¼ tsp. dry mustard
1 tsp. cider vinegar or lemon juice
1 tsp. Worcestershire sauce
About 4 tbsp. mayonnaise
Salt and freshly ground black pepper, to
    taste
Paprika

Cut eggs in half lengthwise; remove yolks. In a small bowl, mash yolks. Add mustard, vinegar or lemon juice, Worcestershire, and mayonnaise, using enough to moisten the mixture. Season with salt and pepper. Spoon the mixture into the egg-white halves. Sprinkle with paprika. Serves 12.

Note: Cut a thin slice from the bottom of each egg-white half so it stands upright.

Rumble Eggs

Marian Cabell Tyree's *Housekeeping in Old Virginia* contains a fascinating variety of inexpensive egg dishes, including this one. The name is typical of many early dishes created by Scottish home cooks, but its origin is unknown.

"Beat up three eggs with two ounces fresh butter or well washed salt butter. Add a teaspoonful cream or new milk. Put all in a saucepan and stir over the fire five minutes. When it rises up, dish it immediately on toast.—Mrs. S."

Ashe County Oat-Cheese Balls

Ashe County, North Carolina, is located in the Blue Ridge Mountains, where many hardy pioneers, including Scottish Highlanders, settled. It has marvelous scenic attractions and the Carolinas' only cheese factory, in West Jefferson, where visitors are welcome to observe the process of making cheeses. During my visit there, a friendly Scottish lady gave me this recipe for a favorite appetizer or snack that she prepares with the local Cheddar.

¼ cup rolled oats (quick or old-fashioned)
½ cup (1 stick) unsalted butter, softened
1 cup finely grated Cheddar cheese
1 tsp. Worcestershire sauce
⅛ tsp. paprika
Salt and freshly ground black pepper, to
    taste

In a small dry skillet over medium-high heat, toast oats, stirring, until lightly browned, about 3 minutes.

In a small bowl, combine butter, cheese, Worcestershire sauce, and paprika. Season with salt and pepper. Mix well. Refrigerate for 30 minutes. Shape into 20 small balls. Roll each cheese ball in oats. Refrigerate, covered with plastic wrap, until ready to serve. Makes 20.

Cheddar-Pecan Roll

This is an attractive cheese specialty that can be easily prepared beforehand and kept several days in the refrigerator until ready to serve. Serve with scones, oatcakes, or soda bread.

1 cup shelled pecans
1 lb. extra-sharp Cheddar cheese, grated
3 oz. cream cheese, softened
¼ cup sour cream
1 tbsp. Dijon-style mustard
1 tsp. paprika
⅓ cup minced green onions
2 tbsp. orange juice or Drambuie

Place pecans on a large piece of wax paper. Fold half the paper over pecans. Crush pecans with a rolling pin. Or crush in a nut grinder or food processor.

In a large bowl, combine cheeses; mash until smooth. Add sour cream, mustard, paprika, green onions, and orange juice or Drambuie. Mix thoroughly. Shape the cheese mixture into a roll about 10 inches long and 2½ inches in diameter. Wrap in wax paper. Refrigerate for about 2 hours, until firm. Place cheese roll over crushed pecans on wax paper to coat it on all sides. Wrap again. Refrigerate for 3 to 6 hours before serving. To serve, cut into thin slices. Makes about 20 slices.

Tillamook Potted Cheese

This specialty may be made with Oregon's Tillamook cheese, ranging in flavor from mild to very sharp, or another favorite Cheddar.

1 lb. Cheddar cheese
3 tbsp. minced green onions
3 tbsp. minced fresh parsley
1 tbsp. Dijon-style mustard
Salt, to taste
2 tbsp. unsalted butter, softened
Dash of Worcestershire sauce
2 tbsp. Scotch whisky

Grate cheese into a small bowl. Add green onions, parsley, mustard, and salt. Mix well. Stir in butter, Worcestershire sauce, and whisky, mixing until creamy. Spoon into a small jar or pot. Refrigerate, covered with plastic wrap, until ready to serve. Serve at room temperature with oatcakes or crackers. Serves 4 to 6.

Helen Lille's Scotch Rarebit

A dear friend, the late Helen Lille, a Scottish-born journalist and author who wrote articles from Washington, D.C., for the *Glasgow Herald*, liked to chat about the proper spelling for this wonderful piquant cheese specialty, which she served for casual entertaining in fall or winter. Made usually of sharp Cheddar cheese cooked with ale or beer and a variety of seasonings, it's called either rarebit or rabbit. Over the years there has been considerable culinary controversy concerning which is correct. Helen maintained that the name should be rarebit from the original "rare-bit," meaning a special dish, and she laughed at the numerous American versions called rabbit and made with all kinds of "strange" ingredients from tomatoes to mushrooms. "In 100 years, preparation of the dish has changed a little because of improved kitchen equipment, but its ingredients remain constant," she wrote.

2 tbsp. unsalted butter
1 lb. sharp Cheddar cheese, coarsely grated
½ tsp. dry mustard
1 tsp. Worcestershire sauce
Dash of cayenne pepper
Salt and freshly ground black pepper, to taste
2 egg yolks, beaten
½ cup light ale
4 slices warm toast

In a chafing dish or double boiler, melt butter over medium-high heat. Add cheese and melt, stirring often in one direction. Add mustard, Worcestershire sauce, and cayenne pepper. Season with salt and pepper, continuing to stir in the same direction. In a small bowl, combine yolks and ale. Add to the cheese mixture, stirring as you do so. Reduce the heat to medium low. Cook, never letting the mixture boil and stirring almost continuously, until the mixture is smooth and velvety. Serve over toast. Serves 4.

Cheese Toast

One of the most notable sayings about this treasured Scottish specialty is from Robert Louis Stevenson's *Treasure Island*, in which the marooned pirate Ben Gunn remarks, "Many's the long night I have dreamed of cheese—toasted mostly."

Many Scottish Americans relish this simple dish as a snack.

White or whole-wheat bread
Butter
Grated Cheddar cheese
Paprika or chopped fresh dill or parsley

Toast bread on one side under a preheated broiler. Butter the untoasted side lightly. Cover with cheese. Sprinkle with a little paprika or a sprinkling of dill or parsley. Put under the broiler until bubbly hot.

Vermont Cheddar-Cheese Pie

This recipe was given to me by a Scottish-American friend who is a resident of the historic mill town and community resort Quechee, Vermont, which has a lively annual Scottish Festival in late August.

The newspaper headlines about one colorful event read, "Scots celebrate their history" and "Quechee Polo Field hosts modern descendants of ancient clans." Tartan kilts were the order of the day as members of the region's clans, about 50, showed their colors. As one woman said, "A lot of people in the Northeast have Scottish blood." But as the newspaper stated, there was "something for everyone at the festival, Scot or not."

6 thin slices bacon
1 unbaked 9-inch pie shell
1½ cups grated Cheddar cheese
3 eggs, beaten
1½ cups light cream
½ tsp. dry mustard
½ tsp. salt
Dash of cayenne pepper

In a small skillet, fry bacon over medium-high heat until crisp. Drain on paper towels; crumble; sprinkle evenly over pie shell. Top with cheese, spreading evenly. In a medium bowl, combine eggs, cream, mustard, salt, and pepper; mix well. Pour into pie shell. In a preheated 375-degree oven, bake for 45 minutes, until a tester inserted into the filling comes out clean. Remove from oven and let set for 5 minutes. Cut into wedges. Serves 6.

Crowdie

A light, moist cottage cheese with a sharp pleasing tang that has been made with leftover skim milk in Scotland's Highlands and Islands since ancient times is a nutritious high-protein and almost fat-free food called crowdie, also spelled crowdy and cruddie. The name comes from an old Gaelic word, *gruth*, for curd.

Relished as a staple food and treasured for its versatility, the cheese is unusual in that it is semicooked or soured naturally, giving it an appealing citric flavor. Eaten fresh, sometimes mixed with cream or butter, or flavored with chopped nuts, fresh herbs, green onions, chives, toasted oats, or fresh fruit or jam, it is a traditional spread for oat and barley breads, scones, and especially oatcakes. Some Scots add crowdie to mashed potatoes; combine a little of it with mayonnaise, lemon juice, and herbs for a salad dressing; or mix it with herbs, garlic, and butter to make a pâté. For a salad, surround a mound of crowdie with sliced raw vegetables and watercress or other greens.

Scottish crowdie is sold in specialty food stores and some Scottish Americans make it in their homes. I have found that a good substitute cheese with a tangy taste and smooth texture can be made with commercial plain yogurt. It must be well drained, however, to obtain the proper consistency. Place the lightly salted yogurt in a sieve lined with cheesecloth and leave it to drain for several hours. Reserve the liquid for cooking or a drink.

Highlands Minted Crowdie

The captivating town of Highlands, nestled in North Carolina's Blue Ridge Mountains, has been called America's Brigadoon, the mythical Scottish village that appeared for one day every century, because of its spectacular location and association with Scots. A popular health resort with several historic landmarks, it is one of the country's most notable and beautiful locations, with inviting dining places and outdoor mountain adventures. This recipe was given to me by a Scottish-American friend after we enjoyed it on a picnic, as Highlands, she said, is a "cheese town," with several shops selling it as well as other delectable foods.

2 cups crowdie or drained low-fat plain
   yogurt
⅓ cup slivered blanched almonds
⅓ cup dried currants
2 tbsp. chopped fresh or 1 tsp. dried mint
Salt and ground white pepper, to taste

In a medium bowl, combine crowdie or yogurt, almonds, currants, and mint. Season with salt and pepper. Mix well. Refrigerate, covered, until ready to serve, up to 2 days. Shape into a mound on a serving plate. Serve with oatcakes. Makes about 2½ cups.

Fish

Scottish Americans are indeed fortunate that our country has a bountiful harvest of fish and shellfish from the blue waters of the surrounding oceans and gulfs, inland lakes, rivers, and streams that provide a great variety throughout the year.

Since their arrival in America, Scots relished fish for daily meals and company fare. The early colonists might not have survived without the abundance of cod in New England, crabs and oysters in Mid-Atlantic locales, trout and whitefish from the Great Lakes, catfish in the South, and salmon and smelts in the Northwest, to name only a few.

In those early days, and for many decades thereafter, the Scottish immigrants were limited to fish and shellfish from local waters. Also, unless salted or otherwise preserved, fish was enjoyed only in season. Today, due to modern transportation, preservation, and packaging, we can relish all varieties from across the land. Fresh, frozen, or canned, the supply is inviting, abundant, and readily available. All is nutritious and offers a welcome change of pace on the menu.

From their forefathers the Scottish Americans inherited a marvelous repertoire of fish recipes. These range from traditional specialties to those devised by housewives and cooks in the United States and Canada. Whether steamed, stewed, broiled, baked, or combined with other foods in delectable dishes, each fish preparation is an inviting creation.

One of the North American locales known particularly for Scottish contributions to fish and shellfish cooking and great dining is the small isle of Cape Breton, "Canada's Scotland," just off the mainland of Nova Scotia. For here the greatest treat is the seafood readily available in coastal fishing villages, town restaurants, hotel dining rooms, and comfortable guesthouses and inns. One is never more than a few miles from the water. If not peerless, the seafood would at least be difficult to match elsewhere. Such is the importance of the fishing industry that the fresh products of the sea and stream are ever evident. Lobster pots dot stony beaches. Small boats with cod line the coasts. Anglers can be spotted along the streams.

Cape Breton's saltwater fish include cod, haddock, pollack, tuna, sea trout, mackerel, halibut, flounder, cunner, smelt, and swordfish. But the most prized product is lobster. During my childhood I had often heard my parents describe the kettles of lobsters, fresh from the sea, which to them were common fare. While visiting the Isle I have had the pleasure of enjoying an appealing selection of lobster sandwiches, grilled lobster rolls, lobster omelets, salads, bisques and chowders, and hot and cold boiled lobsters. Convivial community suppers feature lobsters served whole, or cold in salads with fresh vegetables, or in local homemade foods. 'Tis bonnie good dining.

A marvelous place to enjoy the delectable crustacean is the Lobster Galley at Harbour House, South Haven, with a view of the highlands and St. Ann's harbor. Here the lobster is fresh from an in-house pound, and specialties include Lobster Chowder, Creamy Lobster Bisque, "Larger Ones" for Lobster Lovers, and St. Ann's Cold Lobster Plate (a whole lobster on a bed of fresh salads). The menu includes a section called "How to order and speak in Gaelic."

At St. Ann's Gaelic College of Celtic Arts and Crafts, dedicated in 1938 as a memorial to the island's Highland Scottish pioneers, there are displays and costumed animators who recreate weaving and other traditions and play the bagpipes. The annual Gaelic Mod, held the first week of August, is a celebration of Celtic music, dance, and crafts.

In Indian Brook, population about 60, where my mother, Dolina MacAskill, was born, I once visited a cousin, D. J. MacAskill, who, like many other Islanders, was a fisherman. His coastal storehouse, surrounded by boats, nets, and traps, was filled with barrels of salted cod, kippers, finnan haddie, and other dried and smoked fish, cured in the traditional way with a touch of the elements (dried in the sun, smoked with wood). On the Isle these are favorites, particularly for breakfast. One local specialty that I did not sample was *Ceann Groppe,* Gaelic for boiled cod heads stuffed with cod livers and oats, once a staple morning dish, eaten with bread and a cup of tea.

Scottish settlers who arrived in Cape Breton in the 17th

century began curing fish using salting and smoking techniques acquired in Scotland. They introduced the art of smoked fish, especially salmon, for which Nova Scotia is famous, to Eastern Canada. Scots developed exceptional products, from the everyday smokie (cured haddock) to luxurious smoked salmon, that are still renowned. Smoked fish is important to the diet of the Scots.

Here is a representative collection of Scottish-American fish recipes.

Baddeck Lobster Salad

Baddeck, Cape Breton is a charming community at the beginning of the Cabot Trail. Alexander Graham Bell, born in Edinburgh, Scotland, and famous for inventing the telephone, had a summer home there and worked on his many experiments. One can learn about the scope of his endeavors and inventions by visiting the attractive Alexander Graham Bell National Historic Site, a fitting memorial to the great man, and also by going to his former home, *Beinn Bhreagh* (beautiful hill), three miles from the town, where he and his wife are buried.

Salads made with delectable cooked lobster meat can be simply and elegantly served on lettuce leaves with a topping of plain or lemon-flavored mayonnaise and a garnish of tomato wedges and hard-cooked egg slices.

The lobster may also be combined with shrimp, diced celery, cold, cooked asparagus spears, sliced cold white meat of chicken, or fresh fruit.

This easy-to-prepare salad is especially good for a small luncheon or dinner.

1 lb. cooked lobster meat, cut into ½-inch
   pieces
⅓ cup mayonnaise
2 tbsp. fresh lemon juice
Salt and freshly ground black pepper, to
   taste
Boston or Bibb lettuce leaves, washed and
   dried
2 medium ripe tomatoes, peeled and cut into
   wedges

In a large bowl, combine lobster with mayonnaise and lemon juice. Season with salt and pepper. Serve in a mound on lettuce leaves, garnished with tomato wedges. Serves 4.

Herring

Like their forefathers, Scottish Americans have long relished the nutritious small, bony, humble herring, caught in great quantities in the Atlantic Ocean. Valued for its high protein and low cost, the beloved Scotch food fostered such an important industry that Sir Walter Scott wrote, "It's nae fish ye're buying, it's men's lives."

Scots enjoy herring fresh, smoked, or salted in a variety of good dishes. Fresh, the herring can be potted, pickled, grilled and served with mustard sauce, or fried after rolling in oatmeal.

Some Scottish Americans prepare an old-time dish called Tatties an' Herrin (boiled potatoes topped with herrings and steamed).

Kippers

One of Scotland's most famous and beloved foods is kippers, or kippered herring. They have an distinct taste and Scots around the world like to eat them. Ask a Scottish American about kippers and he will describe them with an eloquence he usually reserves for his favorite whisky. For kippers are revered as a delicacy rather than a commonplace food.

The fish are split open and flattened, then salted, dried, and smoked, acquiring a copper color and desirable strong smoky flavor.

Kippers are eaten fried in butter, baked or poached in milk, or broiled, either plain or perhaps with a butter-lemon sauce. There are delicious kipper sandwiches and spreads. Kippers are added to omelets, served over baked or mashed potatoes, or, in a cream sauce, spooned over toast. Kipper Toast, a favorite for breakfast or High Tea, is made with seasoned mashed or whole broiled kippers, placed on buttered toast, and sometimes topped with a poached egg. Kippers, prepared in a variety of ways, are a favorite Scottish breakfast dish, often served with scrambled eggs and oatcakes.

Kippers soaked in fresh lemon juice overnight, drained, cleaned, and sliced can be eaten like smoked salmon on buttered toast.

In America, plump and golden kippers from Scotland and Canada can be purchased in many specialty food stores. Canned kipper fillets are widely available.

Broiled Kippers

Kippers should be prepared according to package instructions.

1 to 2 kippers
Butter, softened
Freshly ground black pepper, to taste
1 wedge lemon

Place kipper(s) on a broiler rack. Spread with butter and sprinkle with pepper. Broil, according to plumpness, for 3 to 7 minutes, or until the skin curls up and is crisp and brown. Serve with lemon. Serves 1.

Finnan Haddie

Once the butt of jokes by American comedians, finnan haddie, the common name for smoked salted haddock, is a beloved Scottish fish specialty. It comes from the village of Findon (pronounced "Finnan") along Scotland's windswept northeastern coast, where the fisher folk originated the now-famous method of smoking the fish over a peat fire.

Finnan haddie has a pale golden color and soft tender flesh with a mild but assertive smoky flavor. As Etta MacKay, owner of the Scottish Smoked Salmon Co., states, "It's earthy, smoky, and smooth all at once." Scots like it broiled (spread with butter) and served hot and crisp with pats of butter and pepper. There are also those who like the fish poached in milk and served with mustard sauce.

Scottish Americans use cooked and flaked finnans to make creative soufflés and casseroles, to add to scrambled eggs or omelets, to mix with mashed potatoes for fish cakes, and to make creamed dishes, salads, and pâtés. Fried finnans and ham and Egganhaddie (poached fish topped with a poached egg and served with grilled tomatoes) are breakfast specialties.

Here is a favorite Scottish breakfast dish featuring finnan haddie.

¼ cup (½ stick) unsalted butter
2 lb. smoked haddock or finnan haddie,
   skinned and cut into small pieces
Freshly ground black pepper, to taste
4 tsp. cornstarch
2 cups milk
8 hot poached eggs

In a large skillet, melt butter over medium-low heat. Add haddock or finnan haddie. Sprinkle with pepper. Cook for 5 minutes. In a small dish, combine cornstarch with a little milk; add to the fish. Pour in remaining milk. Cook for another 5 minutes. To serve, place eggs over the fish. Serves 8.

Salmon

The succulent salmon, noble in size, graceful in silvery form, and called a "mysterious traveler who inhabits both rivers and the far expanses of the ocean," is a favorite Scottish-American food. Sought after for its delicate flesh and superb flavor, "The King Fish" comes from Pacific and Atlantic waters as well as rivers, including Cape Breton's Margaree River, famous for its trout and salmon. Today most Atlantic salmon sold is farmed, as the wild species is scarce, caught primarily by sport fishermen. Wild Pacific salmon from the Northwest and Alaska is still available and comes in several species, including the highly prized king, sockeye, coho, and chum, as well as pink.

Salmon has a rich flavor and is fine in texture, yet firm and moist. Properly cooked it is a gastronomic treat. The simplest methods of cooking are best: boiling, steaming, baking, grilling (for steaks), or poaching, sometimes served with a sauce.

Sir Walter Scott did not agree, however. For he wrote: "The most judicious gastronomes eat no other sauce than a spoonful of the water in which the salmon has been boiled, together with a little pepper and vinegar."

Morrison's Poached Salmon

There are a number of interesting legends about the Clan Morrison, said to be of Norse origin and descended from a family who were shipwrecked on the shores of the Hebridean Island of Lewis. Two distinct branches evolved—the Morrisons of Lewis and the Morrisons of Harris. The clan society, founded in 1909, has branches worldwide. Those in Canada and the United States are unified under the North American branch of the Clan Morrison Society.

There is no equal to poached fresh salmon, cooked gently in salted water and served with lemon juice and butter or a flavorful shrimp or lobster sauce. It was a great favorite of my cousin Sandy Morrison.

Scale and clean a whole salmon carefully. In a pan large enough to hold the fish, put in enough salted water or a court-bouillon (herbed vegetable or fish stock) to cover the fish. (Measure the thickness of the fish.) Bring just to a boiling point. When the water is hot, add salmon and cook gently over medium-low heat, covered, 10 minutes for every inch of thickness. Remove fish from the liquid. It can be served hot with or without a sauce, and with boiled potatoes, or cold garnished with mayonnaise or Hollandaise and with a cucumber salad.

Smoked Salmon Potato Cakes

As previously mentioned, Scots are very fond of smoked salmon and it is used in a variety of highly prized dishes. Rich and succulent with a distinctly pleasing, smoky flavor, it combines well with mashed potatoes and sour cream to make small cakes coated with toasted oats.

1 lb. (3 medium) red potatoes, peeled
1 tbsp. unsalted butter
3 tbsp. chopped green onions, with some
   tops
1 egg, slightly beaten
2 tbsp. sour cream
½ cup diced smoked salmon
Ground white pepper, to taste
⅔ cup toasted oats*

In a large saucepan, cook potatoes in boiling salted water to cover over medium-high heat for about 18 minutes, until tender. Drain; return to saucepan. Shake over high heat until dry. Turn into a large bowl; mash while still warm.

Meanwhile, in a small skillet, melt butter over medium-high heat. Add onions; sauté 2 minutes. Add to the mashed potatoes. Stir in egg, sour cream, and salmon. Season with pepper. Mix well. Refrigerate, covered with plastic wrap, for 2 to 8 hours.

Sprinkle a pastry board or clean surface with ⅓ cup oats. Turn out the salmon-potato mixture over them. Roll mixture out to about a half-inch thickness. With a floured 2½-inch cutter, cut into 8 rounds. Sprinkle tops with remaining oats. In a buttered large skillet or hot griddle over medium-high heat, cook on both sides, turning once, about 3 minutes on each side, until golden. Serve at once. Serves 8.

*Toast oats in a small dry skillet over medium-high heat until lightly browned, stirring, about 3 minutes.

Oregon Salmon-Potato Salad

In Oregon, superb salmon reigns supreme and Scottish Americans prepare their favorite dishes with the freshly caught fish. But canned wild salmon is also excellent for making this handsomely garnished salad, an appealing entree for a luncheon or supper.

2 cans (1 lb. each) salmon
4 cups peeled, cooked, and diced potatoes
1 cup peeled, diced cucumbers
½ cup diced green peppers
1 medium yellow onion, minced
1 cup mayonnaise
¾ cup sour cream
2 tbsp. fresh lemon juice
1 tsp. dried dill
Salt and freshly ground black pepper, to
  taste
1 head leafy lettuce, washed, dried, and
  chilled
2 hard-cooked eggs, shelled and sliced
2 medium ripe tomatoes, peeled and cut into
  wedges

Remove skin and bones from salmon; break salmon into chunks. Put with potatoes, cucumbers, green peppers, and onions in a large bowl. In a small bowl, combine mayonnaise, sour cream, lemon juice, and dill. Season with salt and pepper. Add to salmon-potato mixture, combining carefully.

To serve, place lettuce leaves on a platter or in a salad bowl. Top with the salad. Garnish with eggs and tomatoes. Serves 8.

Brunswick Salmon Loaf

Brunswick, Maine, is the seat of Bowdoin College and a cultural and trading center for a wide area of inland, coastal, and resort communities. Many Scottish Americans live there, and it boasts a number of inviting salmon dishes, including this typical loaf made with the canned fish and flavored with capers and lemon juice.

A festive time to be in Brunswick is in August, when those of Scottish heritage celebrate at the Maine Highland Games held at Thomas Point Beach.

1 can (1 lb.) salmon, cleaned and flaked
2 cups soft breadcrumbs
½ cup milk
2 eggs, beaten
1 medium yellow onion, minced
2 tsp. drained capers
2 tbsp. fresh lemon juice
½ tsp. crumbled dried rosemary
½ cup chopped fresh parsley
Salt and freshly ground black pepper, to
**   taste**
2 cups hot cooked green peas

In a large bowl, combine salmon, breadcrumbs, milk, eggs, onion, capers, lemon juice, rosemary, and parsley. Season with salt and pepper. Pack into a lightly greased 9 x 5 x 3-inch loaf pan. In a preheated 350-degree oven, bake for 45 minutes, until the loaf is cooked and shrinks from the edges of the pan. With 2 spatulas, transfer the loaf to a serving dish. Cut into slices to serve. Surround with peas. Serves 6.

Pensacola Red Snapper

Historic Pensacola, Florida, home to many persons of Scottish heritage and located on the Gulf of Mexico, is known for its excellent seafood dishes featuring freshly caught fish from the coastal waters. Included among them is red snapper, a lean fish with juicy meat and a delicate flavor that is best baked with citrus juices.

One of the area's legendary characters is Alexander McGillivray, the son of a Scottish trader and a French-Indian woman who became chief of the Creek Indians in the Pensacola region during Revolutionary days. Educated in Charleston and esteemed by George Washington, among other contemporaries, McGillivray negotiated important treaties and was a leading spokesman for Indian tribes along the Florida-Georgia frontier.

2 lb. red snapper fillets or other fish fillets
3 tbsp. vegetable oil
2 tbsp. orange juice
2 tsp. grated orange rind
l tsp. salt
Dash of freshly grated nutmeg and ground
  black pepper

Cut fillets into serving-size portions. Place in a single layer, skin side down, in a well-greased 12 x 8 x 2-inch baking dish.

In a small dish, combine oil, orange juice and rind, salt, nutmeg, and pepper. Pour over fillets. In a preheated 350-degree oven, bake for 25 to 30 minutes, until fish flakes easily when tested with a fork. Serves 6.

Cabbie Claw

Some Scottish Americans who hail from the Shetland Islands in northern Scotland prepare this traditional poached cod dish for special occasions. In the Shetlands, a codling is called *kabbilow*, from the French *cabillaud*, meaning fresh cod.

1 lb. fresh cod fillets
1 cup boiling water
1 tbsp. white vinegar
2 tsp. prepared horseradish, drained
3 tbsp. chopped fresh parsley
Salt and freshly ground black pepper, to
    taste
2 tbsp. unsalted butter
2 tbsp. all-purpose flour
1 cup milk
1 tbsp. Dijon-style mustard
2 hard-cooked eggs, shelled and minced
2 cups warm, seasoned mashed potatoes

Put cod in a large skillet over medium-low heat. Pour in boiling water. Add vinegar, horseradish, and 1 tbsp. parsley. Season with salt and pepper. Simmer, covered, for about 7 minutes, until fish is tender. Strain liquid and reserve. Transfer fish to a serving dish; keep warm.

In a medium saucepan, melt butter over medium-low heat. Stir in flour; cook for 1 minute. Gradually add fish liquid and milk, stirring. Stir in mustard. Season with salt and pepper. Cook, slowly, stirring, until thickened and smooth. Add eggs. Cook for 1 minute. Pour over cod. Sprinkle with remaining parsley. Form a border with potatoes around the dish. Serves 4.

Cape Cod Codfish Cakes

Cod, a nutritious fish found in the colder waters of the North Atlantic, played a historic role in early New England and Canadian coastal settlements where fishing was the main source of income. The plentiful and sturdy fish provided a fresh taste of the sea. Its firm, white, and delicious flesh was used to make a wide variety of dishes such as Kippered Cod, Codfish-Potato Pie, and Thatched Cod (a pastry-covered pie), favored by Scottish immigrants, and its vitamin-rich liver and even the tongues were relished as delicacies. Dried salt cod became a staple food. Codfish cakes are still favorite fare.

1 lb. salt codfish
3 cups sliced potatoes
2 tbsp. unsalted butter
2 eggs, slightly beaten
¼ cup milk
⅛ tsp. grated nutmeg
Freshly ground black pepper, to taste
Unsalted butter or vegetable oil, for frying

Soak codfish in cold water to cover for 2 hours. Drain; shred. Put codfish and potatoes into a medium saucepan. Cover with boiling water. Cook over medium-high heat, covered, for about 30 minutes, until fish and potatoes are tender. Drain and mash in a medium bowl. Add butter, eggs, milk, and nutmeg. Season with pepper. Refrigerate, covered, until ready to cook. Shape into 6 patties. Melt butter or heat oil over medium-high heat, and fry patties for about 3 minutes on each side, until golden. Serves 6.

Chesapeake Bay Crab Cakes

The Chesapeake Bay area of Maryland is famous for its endless supplies of superb shad, rockfish, sturgeon, herring, and especially oysters, clams, mussels, crayfish, and crabs. What cooks have done with these gastronomic treasures has made culinary history. Blue crabs, one of the four principal kinds of crabs taken from the marine waters of the United States, are a Bay specialty, relished particularly in crab cakes.

During the 17th century, the Bay's attractions, including seafood, drew thousands of Scots to the area, who became fishermen and farmers. Many of their descendants celebrate their Scottish heritage at A Chesapeake Celtic Festival, held in October at Furancetown Historical Site in Snow Hill, Maryland.

1 lb. cooked crabmeat, preferably lump,
   flaked and picked over
¼ cup fresh breadcrumbs
¼ cup mayonnaise
1 egg, slightly beaten
1 tsp. Worcestershire sauce
1 tsp. minced fresh parsley
Salt and ground white pepper, to taste
3 tbsp. unsalted butter

In a medium bowl, combine crabmeat, breadcrumbs, mayonnaise, egg, Worcestershire sauce, and parsley. Season with salt and pepper. Form the mixture into 4 cakes about ½ inch thick. In a large skillet, melt butter over medium-high heat. Add crab cakes; sauté for about 3 minutes on each side, until golden. Serve at once. Serves 4.

Annapolis Deviled Crab

Annapolis, Maryland's capital and site of the U.S. Naval Academy, has several places of historic interest, including those associated with Scottish Americans. One of them is the crypt of John Paul Jones at the Naval Academy Chapel. Jones, a Scotsman turned American hero, was a sailor and popular Revolutionary War fighter and was sometimes called "Father of the American Navy," who gave it "its earliest traditions of heroism and victory."

The annual Anne Arundel Scottish Festival and Highland Games are held at the Anne Arundel County Fairgrounds, between Annapolis and Baltimore, in early October.

Deviled crab is a favorite dish in Annapolis and other Chesapeake Bay locales.

3 cups crabmeat, preferably lump, picked
  over
⅛ tsp. freshly grated nutmeg
Salt and ground white pepper, to taste
3 tbsp. fresh lemon juice
1 tbsp. Dijon-style mustard
⅓ cup fresh breadcrumbs
⅓ cup melted unsalted butter

In a medium bowl, combine crabmeat and nutmeg. Season with salt and pepper. Stir in lemon juice, mustard, breadcrumbs, and butter. Spoon into 4 crab shells or individual ramekins. In a preheated 375-degree oven, bake for 20 minutes, until bubbly hot and golden brown. Serves 4.

General Scott's Soft-Shelled Crabs

Gen. Winfield Scott, born in Virginia of Scottish ancestry, was in 1841 appointed commander in chief of the army and in 1852 became a candidate of the Whig Party for the presidency. Although he was known as "Old Fuss and Feathers," he was also respected as the nation's most distinguished gourmet. Everywhere he went in the United States, the general talked about food and its preparation and was even accused by political opponents as having preferences for foreign foods, yet his mind was usually on the bounty of his native land.

Among his favorite foods were soft-shelled crabs from the Chesapeake Bay. Actually regular crabs that are molting in order to grow, they are caught immediately after shedding their hard shell, leaving a soft underskin that is completely edible. The meat is sweet and tender, and the best way to cook them is quickly, sautéed for 5 to 8 minutes on each side, in oil and butter on high heat, seasoned only with salt and pepper. While some Bay cooks toss them in a little seasoned flour or dip them in a batter to seal in the flavor, others say broiling also works well, if the crabs are turned over halfway through to ensure even cooking.

Carolina Shrimp Boil

America's most popular shellfish has long been the shrimp, a ten-legged crustacean that was relished by Scottish Americans who settled along South Carolina's coasts, where shrimp cookery developed extensively. Many of the Scots became fond of steamed and spiced shrimp, prepared by arranging them in layers, with hot sauce, salt, and pepper, in a steamer set over boiling vinegar. When pink, they are served in large dishes with a small container of hot melted butter.

During the summer months, convivial Scottish family and holiday celebrations often center on a shrimp boil, with the crustaceans cooked briefly in a little seasoning and served in the shell, sometimes over a newspaper-covered table. Here is a typical recipe.

3 bay leaves
1 tbsp. whole allspice
1½ tsp. crushed red pepper flakes
2 tsp. whole black peppercorns
2 tsp. whole cloves
2 qt. water
2 medium yellow onions, sliced
6 cloves garlic, peeled
2 lemons, sliced
3 to 4 tbsp. salt
2 lb. peeled, deveined shrimp

Tie bay leaves, allspice, red and black peppers, and cloves in a piece of cheesecloth. In a large kettle, combine water, onions, garlic, lemons, and salt. Add the bag of seasonings. Bring to a boil over medium-high heat. Add shrimp. Cover and return to the boiling point. Reduce the heat to medium low. Cook for 3 to 5 minutes. Remove from the heat. Let stand in the spiced water for 5 minutes. Drain and chill. Serves 6.

Long Island Scallops in Coffins

In the eastern part of the United States, particularly Long Island, the sweet, tender bay scallop is relished in many dishes, including this Scottish specialty. However, sea scallops are more available throughout the United States. The "coffins" in the recipe are baked potato shells.

4 hot large baked potatoes
¼ cup (½ stick) unsalted butter
2 tsp. fresh lemon juice
1 tsp. curry powder
2 tbsp. all-purpose flour
1 cup light cream
Salt and freshly ground black pepper, to
    taste
2 tbsp. minced green pepper
2 cups cooked, diced sea scallops
2 tsp. chopped fresh parsley

Cut a lengthwise slice from the top of each potato. Scoop out potato contents; use for another dish.

In a medium saucepan, melt butter over medium-low heat. Add lemon juice and curry powder; sauté for 1 minute. Stir in flour; cook for 1 minute. Gradually add cream, stirring. Season with salt and pepper. Cook slowly until thickened and smooth. Stir in green pepper and scallops. Cook for 1 to 2 minutes to heat. Carefully spoon scallop mixture into potato shells. Garnish tops with parsley. Place in a shallow baking dish. Bake in a preheated 400-degree oven for 15 minutes, until hot. Serves 4.

Poultry and Game

Scottish Americans have long been devotees of the great variety of poultry and small game, which still have a place of honor on the dining table. The very popular chicken, turkey, duck, as well as the goose, pheasant, partridge, woodcock, quail, or grouse, among others, are used to prepare an interesting and inviting culinary creations.

It was fortunate for the early Scottish settlers in America that there were ample supplies of chicken, the common domestic fowl called by the Scots "cockerel" and "old hen." As in their homeland, the bird was very often boiled, thus providing two courses: soup and the chicken meat. Other dishes, particularly for company, were pot-roast chicken a variety of stuffings, and roast chicken served with bread sauce and gravy.

Stoved Howtowdie is a traditional pot-roast chicken with an oatmeal-onion stuffing. *Howtowdie* means a young chicken that has never laid an egg. A dish called Friar's Chicken, created in Scotland by cooks of the holy orders, is made with a cinnamon-flavored veal and chicken broth, enriched with egg yolks. The eminent author H. V. Morton acclaimed it as a "great and romantic food" and "a dish to banish melancholy."

In America there was also a plentiful supply of the native wild turkey, an ancient bird domesticated by the Aztecs. The handsome birds with rich plumage were, according to one observer, "of an incredible Bigness." From the start, the wild birds were relished for daily meals and there are many early recipes for roast young turkey, as well as boiled and steamed. Later, domesticated turkeys were raised for the superior quality of their meat. Traditional Scottish dishes include Turkey Hash; Deviled Turkey, made with piquant seasonings; and *Roastit Bubbly Jock* (the name for a turkey cock), stuffed with sausage and chestnuts.

As in Scotland, the early settlers enjoyed the bounty of superb wild game, especially deer, and noble birds found in the vast forests and plains. Hunting has long been a favorite Scottish pastime. Birds were often roasted and served with a tart jelly, and game was braised, accompanied by piquant sauces and jellies. There are early Virginia recipes for roast woodcock, partridge, and wild duck, flavored with the juice of oranges or with onions. Venison Collops, thin slices fried in butter and cooked in a spicy sauce, were favorite fare. These dishes all still hold many delights for today's diner.

Over the years, Scottish cooks have taken great pride in serving chicken for special-occasion meals, particularly on Sunday, and turkey has been an honored dish at holiday get-togethers. The Scots have traditionally favored savory pies made with game or birds. Today we have excellent poultry and game that is readily available year round and served for family meals as well as entertaining.

Presented here is a representative collection of poultry and game dishes, with a special emphasis on chicken.

Scotch Fried Chicken

From 1738 until 1800, large numbers of Scottish Highlanders found it expedient to leave their homeland, many of them because they had been supporters of Bonnie Prince Charlie during his failed 1745 venture. Thousands of the Scots settled in North Carolina and, according to historical accounts, Gaelic became so prevalent there that papers were printed and sermons were given in the language. To this day, many local words of mysterious origin, and certain Southern accents, can be traced back to the Gaelic. These Scots brought their recipes with them to the New World too.

For me 'tis a great pleasure to meet a Southerner and mention casually that one of the great Scottish contributions to the American cuisine is fried chicken. The reaction to this statement is almost always one of disbelief. For fried chicken has long been the best-known and -loved Southern dish, now an all-American favorite prepared in many variations across the country.

So how can the Scots take credit for the introduction of fried chicken to the American cuisine? Look back in history. During their famous tour of the Highlands, Dr. Samuel Johnson and his Scottish companion, James Boswell, were served fried pullets on the Isle of Skye in 1773 and wrote about it in their travel books, because at the time chicken was customarily baked or boiled in England and the Lowlands. Thus culinary historians believe that emigrants from Skye, and there were many, introduced the method of frying chicken when they settled in the Carolinas, where the efficient and simple cooking process was readily adapted and spread throughout the South.

In the 1828 edition of *The Virginia Housewife*, Mary Randolph of Scottish ancestry wrote the first known recipe for fried chicken and aptly details what is considered to be the basic technique for frying the chickens: "Cut them up . . . dredge them well with flour, sprinkle them with salt, put them into a good quantity of boiling lard, and fry them a light brown . . . take half a pint of rich milk, add to it a small bit of butter, with pepper, salt, and chopped parsley; stew it a little, and pour over the chickens."

Over the years just about every Southern cook, including Scottish Americans, has adopted a favorite technique and recipe for fried chicken and they are all beloved specialties, often served for family reunions and special events.

Here are two recipes for fried chicken.

Picnic Fried Chicken

This crisp, golden chicken, dipped in buttermilk and lemon juice and coated with a seasoned flour-cornmeal mixture before it is fried, is excellent for a picnic or to bring to the Scottish Games for an outdoor meal.

2 cups buttermilk
2 tbsp. fresh lemon juice
1½ cups all-purpose flour
¾ cup yellow cornmeal
1 tbsp. paprika
1 tbsp. salt
½ tsp. freshly ground black pepper
3 frying chickens, about 3 lb. each
Vegetable oil, for frying

In a shallow bowl, combine buttermilk and lemon juice. In a large brown paper bag, combine flour, cornmeal, paprika, salt, and pepper, shaking well to blend.

Cut chicken into serving pieces, rinse, and pat dry. Working with 1 to 2 pieces of chicken at a time, dip first into the buttermilk-lemon mixture, letting any excess drip back into the bowl, then add to the bag containing flour-cornmeal mixture; shake gently to coat chicken. As each piece is coated, remove to a wire rack, first shaking off any excess mix. Refrigerate chicken on a rack set on a baking sheet for 1 hour.

When ready to fry, pour oil into a large heavy skillet to a depth of ¼ inch; heat over medium-high heat until hot. Add enough chicken pieces to fit in the skillet in a single layer. Cover the skillet; cook until chicken is crisp and golden, about 8 to 10 minutes. Turn with tongs. Fry, uncovered, until crisp and golden, about 10 minutes. Remove to a double thickness of paper towels to drain. Cool at room temperature. Then refrigerate, wrapped in foil. Serve within 2 days, returning to room temperature. Serves 12.

Daniel Boone's Kentucky Fried Chicken

Daniel Boone, the intrepid frontiersman of Scottish heritage known for courageous exploits and establishing the first permanent settlement in Kentucky at Boonesboro in 1775, was said to be fond of fried chicken. According to *The Early American Cookbook*, he stated that "there's no better way to cook young chicken." This recipe is an adaptation of one said to have originated in the family of Daniel Boone.

2 frying chickens, about 2½ lb. each
¾ cup + 2 tbsp. all-purpose flour
¼ tsp. paprika
Salt and freshly ground black pepper, to
    taste
½ cup (1 stick) unsalted butter
¾ cup water
1 cup light cream

Cut chicken into serving pieces, rinse, and pat dry. Dredge in ¾ cup flour seasoned with paprika, salt, and pepper.

In a large heavy skillet, melt butter over medium-high heat. Put in chicken; fry quickly on all sides until golden. Reduce heat to medium low. Add water. Cook chicken, covered, for 30 minutes, until tender. Remove chicken to a hot platter. Stir 2 tbsp. flour into the drippings left in the skillet and blend well. Gradually add cream. Cook over medium-low heat, stirring, until thickened. Season with salt and pepper. Pour the gravy over chicken. Serves 6 to 8.

Happit Hen

According to an old Scots recipe, this dish was made with a tough hen cooked in a liquid with vegetables. *Happit* is the Gaelic word for covered. This is a modern version adapted by a Scottish-American cook.

¼ cup (½ stick) unsalted butter
1 medium yellow onion, minced
2 medium carrots, peeled and chopped
1 cup diced celery
3 tbsp. all-purpose flour
2 cups chicken broth
½ tsp. dried marjoram or thyme
Salt and freshly ground black pepper, to
    taste
½ cup light cream
2 cups diced cooked chicken

In a medium saucepan, melt butter over medium-high heat. Add onion, carrots, and celery. Cook, stirring, until the vegetables are tender, 4 minutes. Stir in flour. Cook for 1 minute. Gradually add chicken broth, stirring. Add marjoram or thyme. Season with salt and pepper. Cook slowly, covered, until thickened and smooth, about 10 minutes. Add cream and chicken. Cook for another 3 to 4 minutes. Serve at once over hot cooked rice, if desired. Serves 4.

Whistler's Mother's Chicken in Cream

James McNeill Whistler, an important American artist of the 19th century and of Scottish ancestry, is famous for the portrait of his mother. Known simply as *Whistler's Mother*, the beloved painting hangs in the Louvre in Paris. Not as well known is that the painter's mother, Anna McNeill Whistler, was a devoted cook and kept a manuscript book of recipes for many years. Bequeathed to the University of Glasgow, the manuscript was edited for publication by Margaret F. MacDonald as *Whistler's Mother's Cook Book*.

This is an adaptation of Mrs. Whistler's recipe for Chickens in Cream as a Scottish friend serves it for a Christmas breakfast. It includes the addition of pimiento.

¼ cup (½ stick) unsalted butter
1 medium yellow onion, minced
2 tbsp. all-purpose flour
2 cups light cream
3 cups diced cooked white meat of chicken
1 can (7 oz.) pimiento, drained and chopped
Salt and freshly ground black pepper, to
     taste
2 tbsp. chopped chives

In a medium saucepan, melt butter over medium-high heat. Add onion; sauté until tender, 4 minutes. Stir in flour; cook for 1 minute. Gradually add cream; cook for 5 minutes. Lower the heat to medium low. Add chicken and pimiento. Cook for 5 minutes Season with salt and pepper. Serve, garnished with chives, over scones. Serves 6.

Clan Donald's Smothered Chicken

The most powerful of all the Highland clans, the Clan Donald takes its name from Donald, grandson of Somerled,

King of the Isles. Lord Godfrey Macdonald, the 34th High Chief of Clan Donald, and his wife, Claire Macdonald, a world-renowned cookbook author, writer, teacher, and lecturer, have a cooking school at Kinloch Lodge, a country-house hotel on the Isle of Skye. They travel frequently to America, where they are both well known, and Claire speaks enthusiastically about the goodness of Scottish foods.

For Scottish Americans, good ol' chicken has always been a favorite standby, as it is inexpensive, everybody likes it, and it can be prepared in a hundred different ways, including a dish that was dubbed "smothered" and cooked variously. Many of the early recipes for it were called "smoored," the Scottish word for smothered.

Members of the Clan Donald U.S.A. are fond of this chicken specialty. This recipe is from a MacDonald friend.

2 frying chickens, about 2½ lb. each
Salt and freshly ground black pepper, to
    taste
½ cup (1 stick) unsalted butter
1½ cups chicken broth
1 lb. fresh mushrooms
1 cup light cream

Quarter the chickens, wash, and wipe dry. Sprinkle with salt and pepper. In a heavy skillet, melt butter over medium-high heat. Add chicken. Sauté, turning, until golden brown on all sides, about 5 minutes. Remove to a baking dish. Add chicken broth to baking dish. Bake, covered, in a preheated 350-degree oven for 1 hour, basting occasionally.

Meanwhile, clean mushrooms with a brush or paper towel. Pull the stems from the caps. Set aside the stems to use for another dish. When chicken has cooked for 1 hour, add the mushroom caps and cream. Cook for another 10 minutes, until chicken is tender. Serve chicken covered with mushrooms and sauce. Serves 6 to 8.

Chicken Stovies

This dish, also called Stoved Chicken, was a Highland dish brought to early America. The word stovies comes from the French *étouffer*, meaning to cook slowly in an enclosed pot. It is one of the many dishes that the Scots inherited from the French during the 17th-century Auld Alliance. Chopped fresh herbs can be added for extra flavor.

1 broiler-fryer chicken, about 3 lb.
4 medium potatoes, peeled and cut into
    thick slices
1 large yellow onion, sliced
Salt and freshly ground black pepper, to
    taste
½ cup (1 stick) unsalted butter, cut into bits
1 cup chicken broth or water

Cut up chicken. In a large heavy skillet or casserole, arrange alternate layers of chicken, potatoes, and onion, sprinkling each with salt and pepper and dotting with butter. Add broth or water. Cover and bring to a boil over medium-high heat. Lower the heat to medium low and cook slowly until the chicken is tender, about 1 hour. Serves 4.

Shenandoah Valley Mince Chicken

Virginia's Shenandoah Valley, a broad and rolling fertile region between the Allegheny and Blue Ridge mountains with towns called Edinburg and Glasgow, was settled by sturdy Scotch-Irish pioneers who brought traditions of hard work with them. They turned land into profitable farms and started small industries. For years the area has been known for its apple orchards, vegetables, beef and dairy cattle, as well as chickens and turkeys.

Many of the Scotch-Irish descendants in the Shenandoah lands continue to enjoy dishes that are plain and nourishing, such as this chicken specialty.

6 tbsp. unsalted butter
2 cups minced raw white meat of chicken
½ cup minced mushrooms
¼ tsp. ground nutmeg
2 tbsp. all-purpose flour
1½ cups chicken broth
Salt and freshly ground black pepper, to
   taste
2 tbsp. chopped fresh parsley
2 tbsp. chopped chives
2 tbsp. light cream

In a small saucepan, melt 2 tbsp. butter over medium-low heat. Add chicken, mushrooms, and nutmeg. Cook, covered, for 5 minutes.

In a medium saucepan, melt remaining butter over medium-high heat. Stir in flour. Cook for about 4 minutes, until thickened and smooth. Add chicken broth. Cook, stirring, about 7 minutes. Season with salt and pepper. Reduce the heat to medium low. Add chicken-mushroom mixture, parsley, chives, and cream. Leave on the stove for about 5 minutes, until hot. Serves 4.

Wet Devil

Deviling, or flavoring with pungent seasonings such as mustard and spices, was a popular old Scottish technique in cooking meats and poultry. This American recipe is for breast of chicken cooked in a flavorful "wet" sauce and is good to serve for a company luncheon or dinner.

½ cup (1 stick) unsalted butter, softened
1 tbsp. Worcestershire sauce
1 tbsp. fresh lemon juice
2 tbsp. Dijon-style mustard
1 tsp. dry mustard
2 tsp. curry powder
Pinch of cayenne pepper
Freshly ground black pepper, to taste
3 whole chicken breasts, cut in halves and
    skinned
2 tbsp. vegetable oil
1 large yellow onion, minced
1¼ cups chicken broth
¼ cup light cream
¼ cup chopped fresh parsley

In a small bowl, cream butter. Add Worcestershire sauce, lemon juice, mustards, curry powder, and peppers. Mix thoroughly.

Pat chicken dry with paper towels. Spread both sides with butter-mustard mixture. Leave at room temperature for 30 minutes.

In a large skillet, heat oil over medium-high heat. Add onion. Sauté until tender, 4 minutes. Add chicken; cook until golden brown on both sides, about 5 minutes. Pour in chicken broth. Lower the heat to medium low. Cook slowly, covered, for 25 minutes, until chicken is tender. Add cream during the last 5 minutes of cooking. Stir in parsley. Serve chicken breasts with the sauce poured over them. Serves 6.

Georgia Country Captain

'Tis said that this version of a curried chicken dish was introduced to Georgia by Scottish settlers who learned about it from army officers returning from service in India. Thus the name became Country Captain. Or, as others claim, it originated in Savannah, a major Atlantic seaport where the original settlers included Scottish men, women, and children who left their Highland homes to help Gen. James Oglethorpe settle the Georgia colony, a buffer between Spanish Florida and British Carolina. Scottish Americans became fond of dishes flavored with spices brought into the seaport, and over the years this chicken curry became a favorite main dish for an outdoor luncheon.

The Savannah Scottish Games and Highland Festival is held at Richmond Hill, Georgia, in April.

1 broiler-fryer chicken, about 2½ lb.
2 to 3 tbsp. curry powder
1 tsp. paprika
Salt and freshly ground black pepper, to
    taste
3 tbsp. vegetable oil
1 large yellow onion, minced
2 cloves garlic, crushed (optional)
1 large green pepper, seeded and chopped
1 can (1 lb.) tomatoes, chopped
½ tsp. dried thyme
3 cups hot cooked rice
½ cup currants or chopped seedless raisins
⅓ cup slivered blanched almonds

Cut up chicken and remove the skin. Pat chicken dry with paper towels. Sprinkle with a mixture of curry powder, paprika, salt, and pepper. Rub gently to press into chicken.

In a large deep skillet, heat oil over medium-high heat. Fry chicken on all sides until golden brown, about 5 minutes.

With tongs remove to a large plate. Add onion and garlic, if desired, to drippings in the skillet; sauté until tender, 4 minutes. Add green pepper, tomatoes, and thyme. Lower the heat to medium low. Cook, uncovered, for 10 minutes. Return chicken to the skillet. Cook, covered, turning once or twice, for about 25 minutes, until chicken is tender. Serve chicken over rice on a platter. Top with the sauce; sprinkle with currants or raisins and almonds. Serves 4.

Chicken Pot Pie

Scottish Americans are fond of main-dish savory pies with a mashed-potato topping. These versatile, substantial dishes can be served hot, barely warm, or at room temperature, without any fuss or bother. This old-time favorite is great for a supper.

⅓ cup unsalted butter
½ cup minced onions
¼ cup all-purpose flour
2 cups chicken broth
¼ tsp. celery salt
Salt and freshly ground black pepper, to
    taste
1 cup cooked green peas
1 cup cooked diced carrots
3 cups cubed cooked chicken
3 cups seasoned mashed cooked potatoes
½ cup shredded Cheddar cheese

In a medium saucepan, melt butter over medium-high heat. Add onions. Sauté until tender, 4 minutes. Stir in flour; blend well. Gradually add chicken broth, stirring, and cook for 5 minutes, until thickened and smooth. Add celery salt. Season with salt and pepper. Remove from the heat. Arrange peas, carrots, and chicken in layers in a 2½-qt. casserole. Cover with the sauce. Top with mashed potatoes. Sprinkle with cheese. In a preheated 425-degree oven, bake for 25 minutes, until bubbly hot. Serves 6.

Monroeville Chicken Salad

Monroeville, Alabama, is the state's literary capital, home to notable author Harper Lee, and was named for our fifth president, James Monroe, of Scottish ancestry. It is one of many towns where Scots settled after moving westward from the Atlantic seaboard.

Two lively state events are the Northern Alabama Scottish Festival, at Dublin Park in Madison in June, and the Alabama Highland Games, at the Alabama Shakespeare Festival Grounds in Montgomery in September.

In Alabama, Scottish-American women like to serve chicken salad, superb in its simplicity, for family wedding receptions, anniversary parties, as well as ladies' luncheons and socials. This is a traditional recipe for the salad.

2 cups diced cooked white meat of chicken
1 cup diced celery
About ½ cup mayonnaise
Salt and freshly ground black pepper, to
    taste
Boston lettuce leaves, washed and dried
Tomato wedges, sliced hard-cooked eggs,
    dill pickles, or capers, for garnish

In a large bowl, combine chicken, celery, and mayonnaise, using as much as desired. Season with salt and pepper. Refrigerate until ready to serve. Serve on lettuce leaves decorated with 1 or more garnishes. Serves 4.

Walnut-Turkey Hash

It was a bright Saturday morning when I visited with some Scottish-American friends in Charleston, South Carolina, and we decided to use some leftover turkey to make hash, a dish of chopped meat or poultry combined with various vegetables and seasonings. Ah! But we just didn't want the plain old-fashioned kind we once enjoyed in our homes. We wished to brighten it up a bit. One lady thought of adding curry powder, another paprika, and I opted for walnuts. For 'tis an old Celtic custom to serve a dish with walnuts on special feast days, as they were believed to bring good luck and good health. So, as we savored the festive dish, that's what we wished to each of the diners.

2 tbsp. unsalted butter
½ cup minced yellow onions
½ cup minced celery
1 tsp. curry powder
½ tsp. paprika
1 cup stale coarse breadcrumbs
4 cups diced cooked turkey meat
½ cup leftover turkey gravy or roasting
    juices from turkey
Salt and freshly ground black pepper, to
    taste
1 cup coarsely chopped shelled walnuts
½ cup heavy cream, room temperature
¼ cup chopped fresh parsley

In a large, skillet melt butter over medium-high heat. Add onions and celery. Sauté until vegetables are tender, 4 minutes. Stir in curry powder and paprika; sauté for 1 minute. Stir in breadcrumbs. Sauté until they begin to brown slightly, about 5 minutes.

Stir in turkey and gravy. Season with salt and pepper. Reduce heat to medium low. Cook, covered, until flavors are blended, about 10 minutes. Stir in walnuts, cream, and parsley. Cook, stirring occasionally, for 5 minutes, until mixture is heated through. Serve at once. Serves 4.

Hunter's Breakfast Braised Quail

Quail, a small migratory game bird with a white flesh, has an appealing, delicate flavor. The young birds can be fried, broiled, roasted, or, as in this favorite Scottish dish, braised with mushrooms and wine.

About ½ cup (1 stick) unsalted butter
4 quail, cleaned
1 lb. fresh mushrooms, cleaned and thickly
    sliced
1½ cups dry white wine
½ tsp. dried rosemary
Salt and freshly ground black pepper, to
    taste
4 rounds buttered white bread

In a large skillet, melt ½ cup butter over medium-high heat. Add quail. Brown in butter on all sides. With a slotted spoon, remove quail to a warm platter. Add mushrooms to the drippings, adding more butter if needed. Sauté for 4 minutes. Remove and set aside. Return quail to the skillet. Add wine and rosemary. Season with salt and pepper. Lower the heat to medium low. Cook, covered, until tender, about 30 minutes. Return mushrooms to the skillet during the last 5 minutes of cooking. Remove quail and mushrooms to a warm platter and keep warm. Fry bread rounds in the warm drippings. Serve each quail over 1 fried bread round. Spoon any remaining gravy over quail. Serves 4.

Tipsy Pheasant

The pheasant, a highly prized, handsome game bird closely related to the partridge and quail, has a tender and highly flavorful flesh, which Scottish Americans relish. Generally roasted with a few flavorings, including herbs and wine, the bird is also used to make rich game pies.

2 young pheasants, 3 to 4 lb. each
Salt and freshly ground black pepper, to
   taste
1 medium yellow onion, peeled and halved
2 thyme sprigs
¼ cup unsalted butter, melted
1 cup dry white wine

Wipe pheasants with a damp cloth. Sprinkle inside and out with salt and pepper. Put an onion half and thyme sprig in the cavity of each bird. Truss the birds. Place breast side up on a rack in a roasting pan. Brush with melted butter. Pour in wine. In a preheated 350-degree oven, roast pheasants, allowing 25 minutes per pound, until tender, basting frequently. Transfer to a warm serving platter. Serve with a tart jelly or bread sauce. Serves 6.

Roast Grouse

The rich dark meat of the grouse, a plump bird of many varieties and related to the pheasant, having brown, red, and gray plumage, has long been prized by the Scots. Although they relish all species of the grouse, gastronomes regard the red grouse as the finest game bird in the world. In Scotland, the "Glorious Twelfth" of August heralds the opening of the British shooting season and is an important social event. It is the time of the first grouse, or "Scotch Grouse."

The foremost American species is the ruffled grouse, which ranges from Minnesota through the New England states and from Pennsylvania to northern Georgia and Alabama.

The succulent grouse meat needs only brief cooking and is best when broiled or roasted. Typical flavorings are cranberries and citrus fruit.

2 young grouse, about 1½ lb. each
Salt and freshly ground black pepper, to
    taste
4 tbsp. unsalted butter, softened
3 tbsp. fresh lemon juice
1 cup cranberries
4 slices bacon
4 slices buttered toast

Rinse birds, drain, and pat dry. Sprinkle inside and out with salt and pepper. In a small dish, combine butter and lemon juice. Add to cranberries and put mixture inside each bird cavity, dividing evenly. Place birds breast side up in a roasting pan. Cover the breast of each bird with 2 bacon slices. Fasten with wooden picks. In a preheated 350-degree oven, roast birds for about 40 minutes, until tender. Remove from the oven. Take off bacon. Serve birds on buttered toast rounds and garnish with parsley or watercress sprigs, if desired. Serves 2.

Minnesota Venison Pot Roast

Minnesota, an immense and rich agricultural state noted for its abundance of fish, dairy products, and excellent game, including deer, attracted Scottish settlers looking for lands to farm. One of their favorite foods was venison, deer meat, which is best marinated and pot-roasted in order to tenderize it.

American Scots celebrate their ancestry at the Minnesota Scottish Fair & Highland Games at the Dakota County Fairgrounds in Farmington in early July.

1 venison shoulder roast, 4½ to 5 lb.
1 clove garlic, halved
2 cups dry red wine or cranberry juice
2 slices lemon
1 large yellow onion, sliced
1 bay leaf
2 parsley sprigs
Salt and freshly ground black pepper, to
  taste
3 tbsp. vegetable shortening or oil
1 cup sour cream

Put venison into an earthenware crock or non-aluminum deep container. Cover with garlic, wine or juice, lemon slices, onion, bay leaf, and parsley. Season with salt and pepper. Refrigerate, covered, for 1 to 2 days, turning once or twice. Take from marinade; pat dry with paper towels. Strain and reserve marinade. In a heavy kettle, heat shortening or oil over medium-high heat. Add venison; brown on all sides. Add reserved marinade. Lower the heat to medium low. Cook slowly, covered, for about 3 hours, until venison is tender. Slice and keep warm. Scrape the drippings. Add sour cream. Heat slowly for 5 minutes. Pour over venison. Serves 8.

Stuffings

Scottish-American recipes for subtly seasoned mixtures to use as stuffings—or, as they were once called, dressings—for poultry and game birds are creative and delectable, inspired by traditional and contemporary specialties. For the Scottish cook has long known that "for every season she hath dressings fit."

Because stuffing expands considerably during cooking, it should be packed loosely. Allow about 1 cup of stuffing per pound of meat. Although the stuffing may be prepared beforehand and refrigerated, it should be inserted into the bird just before cooking. Any excess stuffing can be baked separately.

Here are two typical recipes.

Apple Stuffing

3 cups peeled, chopped tart apples
2 cups minced yellow onions
2 tbsp. fresh lemon juice
2 tsp. grated lemon zest
6 cups day-old soft bread cubes
½ tsp. dried thyme
Salt and freshly ground black pepper, to
    taste

In a large bowl, combine apples, onions, lemon juice and zest, bread, and thyme. Season with salt and pepper. Refrigerate, covered, until ready to use. Makes about 10 cups.

Sage-Onion Stuffing

This is a good stuffing for duck, chicken, or turkey.

½ cup (1 stick) unsalted butter
2 cups minced yellow onions
1 cup minced celery with some leaves
6 cups day-old soft bread cubes
1 tbsp. crumbled dried sage
½ cup chopped fresh parsley
Salt and freshly ground black pepper, to
   taste

In a small skillet, melt butter over medium-high heat. Add onions; sauté until tender, 4 minutes. Turn into a large bowl. Add celery, bread, sage, and parsley. Season with salt and pepper. Toss to thoroughly combine. Refrigerate until ready to use. Makes about 10 cups.

Meats

Among the gastronomic delights that grace Scottish-American tables, meats are treasured and very often the stars of family and company meals. The diverse selection of excellent national favorites and innovative creations made with beef, lamb, veal, pork, and variety meats appeals to all tastes.

Scottish Americans have been dedicated meat eaters since their arrival in the New World. They are also inventive in using the flesh as well as many parts of the animals, together with compatible ingredients, in the preparation of distinctive dishes.

As in their homeland, the most favored meat of the early Scots was mutton, the flesh of sheep that was generally boiled, baked, roasted, or barbecued. Over the years, however, Scots would grow to prefer sweet-tasting lamb, usually in the form of a roast served with red currant or mint jelly; as chops, fried or broiled; and cut up to make stews. Early dishes of meat cubes with vegetables, sometimes legumes, and seasonings, provided necessary sustenance and were made in fascinating variety, popular for informal meals.

Scots are also fond of beef from their superior Galloway and Aberdeen Angus cattle. The celebrated "Roast Beef of Old England" has, for generations, been Scottish in origin. After the cattle were introduced into America, various cuts of Scotch beef, especially steaks and roasts, have been and still are highly rated for their quality. As the saying goes, "Scotch beef is more than a little bit special."

The Scottish-American tradition of making small amounts of food go a long way and of utilizing leftovers has resulted in superb Scotch puddings, loaves, meatballs, and pasties, especially one commonly called a *bridie*. A pastry turnover with a beef filling, it came from Forfar in Angus, where it is said to have been the creation of a baker known as Mr. Jolly. Once sold at farmers' markets, these pasties are now popular fare at Highland Games and Gatherings. A *bridie* with one hole has only meat inside; one with two holes includes onions also.

One of the most important meats from imported domestic animals was pork. Pigs were easy to transport to the New

World, and they were welcomed in small Eastern communities. Pigs were fed acorns and nuts, and the colonists learned from the Indians how to dry-cure and smoke their hind legs. Thus Scottish Americans, along with the English settlers, were soon producing what became the famous Smithfield ham, named for a small town along the James River in the Tidewater region, where farmers lived and worked. According to one of them, a Southern saying was: "A good Virginia ham ought to be spicy as a woman's tongue, sweet as huh kiss, an' tender as huh love."

Baked, spiced Virginia ham was favorite fare at Thomas Jefferson's Monticello, and in *The Virginia Housewife*, Mary Randolph gave us one of the earliest ham recipes: "TO STUFF A HAM: Take a well smoked ham, wash it very clean, make incisions all over the top two inches deep, stuff them quite full with parsley chopped small and some pepper, boil the ham sufficiently; do not take off the skin. It must be eaten cold."

Over the years many other states, notably North Carolina, Georgia, Tennessee, and Kentucky, became well known for their country hams, cured by the application of salt and usually smoking as well.

Philip Danforth Armour, a Scottish American, was born in 1832 on the family farm in upstate New York and left for the California Gold Rush at age 19. During the Civil War, he started a grain business in Chicago and then opened Armour Meats, which by 1923 was the largest meat packer in the world. Among his catchy marketing ideas was suggesting that ministers would preach better "if they included more of Armour's sausages in their diet."

McDonald's, the world's most successful and extensive restaurant empire, now in some 115 countries on six continents and with new ones opening each year, was founded by the Irish-American McDonald brothers, Richard and Maurice, whose parents are said to have come from County Kerry. "Most of the Irish McDonalds are ultimately descended from Scottish gallowglasses (foreign soldiers)," wrote Duncan A.

Bruce in *The Mark of the Scots*. *MacDhomhnaill* is the name in Gaelic.

According to a Scottish newspaper item, residents in Fort William, Scotland, have been struggling for years to persuade McDonald's to recognize their Scots origin, "insisting that the company's founders are direct descendants of a Lochaber family who emigrated from Fort William in 1820." A spokesman for the company stated that they were "looking into the matter."

McDonald's has had an enormous impact around the world, affecting daily eating and customs. The Big Mac, which arrived in 1968 and cost 49 cents, has found its way onto international menus and is still a great favorite. Although the Scots did not create the hamburger, as it is now known, they have long enjoyed a number of dishes made with ground or minced meat.

Scottish-American cooks have a special talent for preparing meats in a number of appealing dishes, many with fascinating backgrounds and amusing names. The following selection includes some of the best of them.

Aberdeen Angus Whisky Steaks

A breed of black hornless steers called Aberdeen Angus or Black Angus, originally bred in the counties of Aberdeen and Angus in Scotland, was brought to the United States and in a short time replaced the longhorn as the preferred beef steer. A Scot, George Grant, introduced "the freaks because of their lack of horns and jet black color" at the Kansas City Livestock Show in 1873. The massive, meaty Black Angus provided the leading source for what is called Scotch beef.

¼ cup (½ stick) unsalted butter
1 large yellow onion, cut crosswise and
    thinly sliced
4 center-cut filet steaks
½ cup beef broth
½ tsp. freshly ground black pepper
¼ cup Scotch whisky

In a large skillet, melt butter over medium-high heat. Add onion slices; sauté until tender, 4 minutes. Remove to a plate and keep warm. Add steaks to the drippings and sear over high heat for 1 minute on each side. Reduce heat to medium low and cook steaks for about 4 minutes on each side for medium rare. Remove to warm plates.

Increase the heat to medium high. Add broth, stirring and scraping up all the browned bits on the bottom. Cook for 2 to 3 minutes, until the liquid is reduced by half. Season with pepper. Add whisky. Heat for 1 minute. Pour over steaks. Garnish with onions. Serve with a pat of butter on top of each, if desired. Serves 4.

Mince and Tatties

A popular Scottish everyday or supper dish called mince, a colloquialism for ground or "minced" meat, is usually served with mashed potatoes, or *tatties*. Some Scots say that mince is the Scottish hamburger, but it is not made like the American specialty.

1 tbsp. beef drippings or unsalted butter
1 medium yellow onion, minced
1 lb. lean ground beef
½ cup beef broth
1 tbsp. rolled oats
1 tbsp. Worcestershire sauce
Freshly ground black pepper, to taste
Mashed potatoes

In a large skillet, heat drippings or melt butter over medium-high heat. Add onion. Sauté until tender, 4 minutes. Add beef; brown quickly, stirring, until the redness disappears. Lower the heat to medium low. Add broth, oats, and Worcestershire sauce. Season with pepper. Cook slowly, covered, for 15 minutes. Serve with potatoes. Serves 4.

Scotch Hamburgers

Chopped or ground meat, shaped into patties or other forms and cooked in various ways, is an ancient specialty. Since a broiled or fried ground-beef patty served on a bun and called a hamburger made its debut at the St. Louis World's Fair in 1904, it has become an all-American favorite.

Many Scottish Americans have their favorite burgers, including this one, which can be embellished by sprinkling a dram or two of Scotch whisky over them after they are cooked.

1½ lb. lean ground beef
Salt, to taste
1 tbsp. unsalted butter (optional)
Freshly ground black pepper, to taste
3 split, toasted hamburger buns or scones
Hot sautéed sliced onions and herbed mushrooms, pickle slices, Worcestershire sauce,
   or chopped fresh dill, for garnish

Shape beef, preferably freshly ground, into 6 patties. Sprinkle a large heavy skillet with a layer of salt and heat over medium-high heat. Add the patties and sear on one side; turn with a spatula. Reduce the heat to medium low and continue cooking patties until done, several minutes. Or omit salt and heat butter in the skillet. Cook patties, turning once, until done. Do not pat or press with a spatula during the cooking. Or cook under a preheated broiler, turning once. Season with salt and pepper and serve open face on buns or scones with any of the garnishes. Serves 6.

Kansas Meatloaf

During the 18th century, many crofters, farmers facing economic problems in Scotland, left their homeland and emigrated to America hoping to reach Kansas, where they could own inexpensive fertile land. According to historical accounts, one of the areas where they settled and farmed came to be called the "Scotch Plains."

McPherson, Kansas, a county and city named for Gen. James Birdseye McPherson, a Civil War hero who died in the Battle of Atlanta in 1864, has been called an "almost Scottish" community. Scots celebrate their heritage at the McPherson Scottish Festival and Highland Games held at Lakeside Park in McPherson on the fourth weekend in September.

Scottish Americans have long been fond of loaves prepared with well-seasoned ground-meat mixtures, traditionally served hot or cold for home meals and picnics at Scottish Games and Gatherings.

2 lb. meatloaf mixture (beef, veal, and pork)
1 cup soft breadcrumbs
½ cup milk
½ cup minced yellow onions
½ cup minced celery
2 eggs, beaten
½ cup chopped fresh parsley
1 tsp. dried herbs (savory, basil, sage, or
    marjoram)
Salt and freshly ground black pepper, to
    taste
3 thin slices bacon

In a large bowl, combine meatloaf mixture, breadcrumbs, milk, onions, celery, eggs, parsley, and herbs. Season with salt and pepper. Mix thoroughly. Pack into a lightly greased 9 x 5 x 3-inch loaf pan. Top with bacon. In a preheated 350-degree oven, bake for 1 hour, until loaf shrinks slightly from the edges of the pan. Pour off any drippings. With 2 broad spatulas, transfer loaf to a serving dish. Cut into thick slices. Serves 6.

Oat-Mushroom Meatloaf

This is an attractive, nutritious meatloaf to serve for a company meal.

½ lb. fresh mushrooms, brushed clean
3 tbsp. unsalted butter
1 cup minced yellow onions
1 tsp. dried dill
2 lb. lean ground beef
¾ cup rolled oats
2 eggs
½ cup sour cream
2 tbsp. Worcestershire sauce
1 tbsp. Dijon-style mustard
1 tsp. prepared horseradish
Salt and freshly ground black pepper, to
    taste
3 tbsp. chopped fresh dill

Cut any tough stem ends from mushrooms; slice thinly lengthwise.

In a medium skillet, melt 2 tbsp. butter over medium-low heat. Add ½ cup onions; sauté for 2 minutes. Add half the mushroom slices; sauté for 4 minutes. Remove from the heat. Add dill.

In a large bowl, combine beef, remaining onions, oats, eggs, sour cream, Worcestershire sauce, mustard, and horseradish. Season with salt and pepper. Mix thoroughly. Spoon half the mixture into a lightly greased 9 x 5 x 3-inch loaf pan. With the back of a large spoon, make a wide indentation lengthwise along the center of the meat mixture. Turn onion-mushroom mixture into the indentation, spreading evenly. Top with the remaining meat mixture, spreading evenly. Press down firmly.

In a preheated 350-degree oven, bake for 1 hour, until loaf shrinks slightly from the edges of the pan. Pour off any drippings. With 2 broad spatulas, transfer loaf to a serving dish.

Meanwhile, in a small skillet, melt remaining butter over medium-low heat. Add remaining mushroom slices; sauté for 4 minutes. Spoon on top of the meatloaf. Sprinkle with fresh dill. Cut into thick slices. Serves 6 to 8.

Collops-in-the-Pan

Collop is an old Scottish word for a thin slice of meat, usually veal or beef, that is cooked in a piquant sauce. In Scotland the *collops* or slices are sometimes minced before cooking and then known as "minced *collops*." Oats are added in this recipe.

3 tbsp. rolled oats
1 lb. top round steak
Salt and freshly ground black pepper, to
    taste
2 tbsp. unsalted butter
1 medium yellow onion, thinly sliced
1 cup beef broth
1 tbsp. Worcestershire sauce
⅛ tsp. freshly grated nutmeg
2 tbsp. chopped fresh parsley, for garnish

In a small skillet, toast oats over medium-high heat, stirring, until lightly browned, about 3 minutes. Remove from the skillet and cool.

Cut off any fat from steak. Slice steak into escalopes, or thin slices, about 3 inches square. Sprinkle with salt and pepper.

In a large skillet, melt butter over medium-high heat. Add

steak squares; brown on both sides. Remove to a plate. Add onion slices to the drippings; sauté until tender, 4 minutes. Return steak to the skillet. Add broth, Worcestershire sauce, and nutmeg. Stir in oats. Lower the heat to medium low. Cook, covered, for 10 minutes. Garnish with parsley. Serves 4.

Inky Pinky

If you want to entice some friends to come for an informal meal, mention that you're serving Inky Pinky. But don't say that it's a hash made with leftover cooked meat. The name alone will be the attraction. Nobody seems to know where the name came from, but a recipe for it was published in a Scottish cookbook in 1826.

2 tbsp. unsalted butter
1 medium yellow onion, minced
1½ cups beef gravy
1 tbsp. red-wine vinegar
Salt and freshly ground black pepper, to
    taste
3 cups cubed cooked beef
1 cup diced cooked carrots
2 tbsp. chopped fresh parsley

In a medium skillet, melt butter over medium-high heat. Add onion; sauté for 3 minutes. Add gravy and vinegar. Season with salt and pepper. Heat to boiling. Reduce the heat to medium low. Add beef and carrots. Cook slowly, covered, for 10 minutes. Stir in parsley. Serve over hot buttered toast slices, if desired. Serves 4.

Scotch Meat Pies

Scottish Americans inherited a fondness for meat pies from their forefathers. As in Scotland, hot meat pies kept out the cold during the winter, and in the summer cold meat pies became standard fare for picnics, outdoor meals, and Scottish Games and Gatherings.

Here are two typical recipes for them.

Angus's Shepherd's Pie

Angus, a first or surname said to be that of an old Celtic god and meaning "one choice," is a former county in Scotland. Like my father, many Scottish Americans were called Angus.

Scots have long been fond of an old dish known as shepherd's pie, made of cut-up cooked meat, usually lamb or beef, mixed with vegetables, gravy, and a little seasoning, put into an ovenproof dish, and covered with a thick layer of mashed potatoes before being baked. It was once taken by shepherds to the hillsides and heated over a wood fire as they watched their sheep.

This easy-to-prepare pie is named for all of the people I've known who were or are called Angus, including my mother's cousin, the Giant Angus MacAskill.

2 cups cut-up cooked Scotch beef
2 cups brown gravy
1 cup sliced cooked carrots
1 cup cooked green peas
1 can (1 lb.) small white onions, drained
2 cups seasoned mashed potatoes
1 egg yolk, beaten

In a medium saucepan, combine beef, gravy, carrots, peas, and onions over medium-high heat. Heat for 2 minutes to blend flavors. Spoon the mixture into a 2¹/₂-qt. casserole dish. In a medium dish, combine potatoes and egg yolk. Arrange in a ring around the edge of the casserole. In a preheated 400-degree oven, bake for 20 minutes, until bubbly hot and golden on top. Serves 4.

Tuppeny Struggles

This is what is called a Scottish version of shepherd's pie. It is made with cubed cooked lamb and flavored with curry powder.

4 tbsp. unsalted butter
2 tsp. curry powder
1 medium yellow onion, minced
2 cups brown gravy
1 tbsp. Worcestershire sauce
½ tsp. dried marjoram
Freshly ground black pepper, to taste
3 cups cubed cooked lamb
2 cups seasoned mashed potatoes
Paprika

In a medium saucepan, melt 2 tbsp. butter over medium-high heat. Add curry powder and onion. Sauté until tender, 4 minutes. Add gravy, Worcestershire sauce, and marjoram. Season with pepper. Lower the heat to medium low. Cook for 5 minutes to blend flavors. Stir in lamb. Cook for another 5 minutes. Spoon into a 2¹/₂-qt. casserole dish. Top with potatoes, spreading evenly. Dot the top with the remaining butter. Sprinkle lightly with paprika. In a preheated 400-degree oven, bake for about 25 minutes, until bubbly hot and golden on top. Serves 4.

Cranberry Pot Roast

Early Scottish settlers in eastern locales of Massachusetts such as Andover and Saugus, the site of the so-called Scotch House, discovered that the bright-red, tart cranberry was an appealing and versatile addition to many dishes, including pot roasts.

1 boneless beef pot roast, 3½ to 4 lb.
3 tbsp. all-purpose flour
Salt and freshly ground black pepper, to
   taste
3 tbsp. vegetable shortening or oil
½ cup water
2 cups strained, cooked cranberry sauce
4 whole cloves
1 cinnamon stick

Wash and wipe beef dry. Season flour with salt and pepper and rub on all sides of beef. In a heavy pot, heat shortening or oil over medium-high heat. Add beef; brown on all sides. Put a rack into the pot under beef. Add water, cranberry sauce, cloves, and cinnamon. Reduce the heat to medium low. Cook slowly, covered, for about 2½ hours, until beef is tender. Slice beef and keep warm. Strain the sauce and pour over beef. Serves 6 to 8.

Patrick Henry's Hotchpotch

Patrick Henry, the son of an immigrant from Aberdeen, Scotland, was one of the great men of Scottish origin who rose from very humble beginnings to become one of the most prominent and influential founders of our country. Having failed successively in farming and "store keeping," he undertook the profession of law and developed his talent of public speaking. He is remembered as an American patriot and orator, member of the Continental Congress, and Virginia's first governor.

Scotchtown, one of Virginia's oldest plantation houses, built in 1719 on the site of a town called Scotch Town established for Scottish settlers, was purchased by Patrick Henry in 1770. He lived there with his family during his most active political years, until 1778. Located north of Richmond and open to the public, the restored house includes furnishings associated with the Henry family. It was also the childhood home of Dolley Payne, who married James Madison.

One of the earliest traditional dishes brought by the Scots to the South was a hearty stew made of lamb and several vegetables in season. Also called harvest pot, this one-dish meal is famous in song and story. A ditty called "A Song in Praise of Hodge Podge" mentions a long list of ingredients. *Housekeeping in Old Virginia*, published in 1879 and written by Marian Cabell Tyree, the granddaughter of Patrick Henry, has a fascinating collection of recipes from 250 famous families of Virginia. Her recipe for hotchpotch is typical of the dish made at that time: "During the summer season get lamb chops, which half fry. Cut up cabbage, lettuce, turnips, onions and any other vegetables, which boil, with seasoning of pepper, salt, etc; one hour before dinner, put in the lamb chops, with some green peas; boil the potatoes separately."

Here is a modified version of the dish.

3 lb. neck or breast of lamb, cut up
Salt and freshly ground black pepper, to
  taste
1 cup water
2 large carrots, peeled and sliced
2 large yellow onions, quartered
2 cups green peas
6 green onions, sliced
1 tsp. sugar
1 tbsp. chopped fresh mint

In a large heavy saucepan over medium-high heat, brown

lamb on all sides. Pour off the fat. Season with salt and pepper. Add water. Lower the heat to medium low. Cook, covered, for 1 hour. Add carrots and onions. Continue cooking for 30 minutes. Add peas, green onions, sugar, and mint. Cook for about 20 minutes, until lamb and vegetables are cooked. Serves 4 to 6.

North Carolina Barbecue

In the South, the ritual of the barbecue, a social entertainment at which meats are roasted over an open fire, has been likened to a "folk ceremony," with chauvinistic participants defending their state, regional, and family traditions with pride and gusto.

As early as the 17th century, when Scottish immigrants settled in Virginia, pork was a favorite meat. It became a common practice to roast whole pigs over hot coals for outdoor meals, which were called barbecues. Gradually, the custom flourished throughout the South, and these became large gatherings at which chicken, beef, lamb, sausages, fish, shellfish, ham, or pork were featured. Most were basted with or dipped in spicy sauces that ranged from mild to hot to hot hot.

In the South, the word barbecue can provoke more heated discussion than any other single topic of food conversation, including fried chicken. Although there are many superb kinds, prepared in countless forms, one of the best and most interesting is the down-home pork barbecue of North Carolina enjoyed in pork houses—informal eateries found in towns and remote locales—particularly in central and northeastern areas. Rocky Mount claims to be "The Barbecue Capital of the World" and Lexington "The Spiritual Center," but you can also find no-nonsense eating in Scotland Neck, Wilson, Goldsboro, Raleigh, and Greensboro, among other locales.

In North Carolina, you will be served pork that is sliced or chopped with a pepper-vinegar sauce, or perhaps a pork-barbecue sandwich. According to the Scots living in the state, the best advice is to enjoy all the regional barbecues at community gatherings or clan meetings, and let the cooks argue their respective merits.

For an informal home luncheon or supper that can be easily prepared in the kitchen, serve a barbecue menu starring this specialty.

1 boneless pork loin, about 5 lb., tied
Salt and freshly ground black pepper, to
    taste
1 cup cider vinegar
1 cup ketchup
1 tsp. paprika
¼ tsp. cayenne pepper

Rub pork with salt and pepper. Place on a rack in a baking pan. In a preheated 450-degree oven, roast for 10 minutes. Reduce heat to 300 degrees. Roast, turning loin 2 or 3 times during cooking, for about 4½ to 5 hours, until thoroughly cooked. Remove from oven.

Meanwhile, combine remaining ingredients in a small saucepan over medium-high heat. Season with salt and pepper. Bring to a boil. Reduce heat to medium low. Cook for 2 to 3 minutes. Remove from the heat. Reheat to serve warm.

To serve the barbecue, slice the meat and serve warm, topped with some warm sauce and with favorite accompaniments. Or chop the meat into small cubes and serve as a filling, topping with some of the sauce and a spoonful of coleslaw, for sandwiches on hamburger buns. Serves 8.

Frank's All-Night "Meat Feast"
of Charcoal Boston Butt

Frank R. Shaw of Atlanta, Georgia, is an active Scottish American, proud of his heritage and "Scottishness," including Scotch fare. An FSA Scot (Fellow of the Society of Antiquaries of Scotland), he is past editor of *Clach na Faire (Stone of the Watch)*, the Clan Shaw newsletter; book reviewer and columnist for *The Family Tree*; president of The St. Andrew's Society of Atlanta; and member of the Burns Club of Atlanta, among other organizations. He is an authority on Robert Burns, boasting a large collection of books on the poet and often writing and lecturing about his life and works. Frank is also an active member of the Clan Shaw Society and contributor to their newsletter, *An Biodag (The Dagger)*, edited by Meredith L. Shaw of Olney, Maryland, the society's president.

This is Frank's recipe, which he prepares with his wife, Susan, for family, friends, and the annual Burns Club potluck dinner.

1 Boston butt, 7 to 8 lb.
Garlic powder
Salt and freshly ground black pepper, to taste

You will need a covered grill large enough to build a charcoal fire at one end and use the other end of the grill to cook the meat indirectly. Enough charcoal should be added for the heat to last about 8 hours. It is best to have a metal container (1 to 1½ gallon size) to put the charcoal in to help prevent it from burning out too quickly. This usually gives you a temperature of around 200 degrees.

Get the charcoal going, put Boston butt on the grill around midnight (see instructions below), go to bed, and take it up the next morning around 8:00. Only the dreams of this "meat feast" should interrupt your sleep. Always allow 7 to 8 hours on the grill. (If you want the meat hot off the grill for dinner, cook it during the day.) It is preferable to serve at room temperature.

To get started, season the meat liberally with garlic powder, salt, and pepper. Place it on the end of the grill away from the heat. After about 1 hour, check to see if the meat has reached a golden color. In order to preserve the slow heat from the charcoal, do not open the grill too often.

Wrap the meat loosely but securely in aluminum foil. Leaving the pork loosely wrapped with a little space at the top allows the meat juices to flow around the meat and gives room for steam to cook it uniformly.

Place the meat back on the end of the grill away from the heat. (Hint: Take another piece of aluminum foil a little bigger than the size of the wrapped meat. Place it on the grill to rest the wrapped meat on. This helps prevent the foil wrapping the bottom of the meat from tearing or developing little holes and losing meat juices.) Close the grill; let the meat cook until morning. Do not open the grill until ready to remove the meat. If not in a hurry to prepare the barbecue, leave it on the grill. The meat juices will continue to keep it warm for about 2 hours.

Prepare the meat by shredding the fat from the butt. The tender pork should pull away easily from the fat and bone. Pull the meat apart into bite-size pieces. Serve the "pulled pork" as is or with a favorite homemade or commercial barbecue sauce. Serves 8 to 10.

Andrew Jackson's Ham with Red-Eye Gravy

Andrew Jackson, the courageous frontiersman, famous army general, and seventh U.S. president, whose father was Scotch-Irish, spent much of his life in Tennessee and retired to a home, the Hermitage, there. He was called "the prince of hospitality" because he entertained a great many people and served good food, including Southern "victuals." He was particularly fond of ham.

According to folklore, it was President Jackson who told a whisky-drinking cook to bring him some ham with gravy that was as "red as your eyes." Thus came about the popular "red-eye" gravy, served over ham as well as toast, grits, or eggs. Another theory is that the gravy acquired its name from the red color of the ham juice. We Scots like to believe the Jackson story.

Made with ham drippings, a piece of ham fat, and a cup of coffee, the gravy is a great favorite in Virginia, North Carolina, Kentucky, as well as Tennessee. This is a typical recipe.

1 slice country-cured ham, 6 to 8 oz.
1 cup strong brewed black coffee

Cut the fat from the edges of ham and rinse ham with warm water to remove any excess salt. In a heavy skillet, sauté ham over medium-high heat until nicely browned. Remove from the skillet. Cut into 2-inch squares and keep warm. Add coffee to pan drippings. Bring to a boil. Stir well and spoon over fried ham. Serves 2.

Haggis

"Fair fa your honest sonsie face,/Great chieftain o' the Pudding race!"

Ever since Robert Burns immortalized Scotland's controversial and beloved national dish in his satirical ode, "Address to the Haggis," nearly everyone seems to have heard of this much-maligned, unpretentious, and earthy concoction. But few people know what it is. They just like to tell jokes about the mysterious creation.

The name gives a clue. While some persons have supposed that this comes from the French *hacher*, to chop, it is mostly believed to have derived from the Scottish word *hag*, meaning to hack. Some Scottish culinary writers maintain that haggis began with the Vikings in Scandinavia.

Haggis is actually an ancient "super-sausage" made traditionally in a boiled sheep's paunch stuffed with a mixture of chopped suet, onions, a sheep's pluck (heart, liver, and lungs), oats, and seasonings.

Scottish postcards picture haggis as a curious short-legged Highland animal hooked on a line or in flight. "First catch your haggis," a Scot will laughingly tell you. And then there are tall tales about a beast *haginasus* that was hunted by the ancient Picts, who used the haggis hound to flush it from the heather. In America, comedians have described haggis as a "boiled bagpipe" and "giant teabag."

'Tis a pity to have the description before the tasting. It is the name and the ingredients of haggis that give it such a bad reputation. There is no doubting Scottish Americans' real fondness for haggis. "Oh what a glorious dish," one of them will say with a twinkle in his eye, knowing that you don't believe him.

In America, it is not possible to prepare a traditional haggis, as U.S. Department of Agriculture regulations prevent the importation of a sheep's stomach and animal lungs in products meant for human consumption. Thus there are many local homemade variations. Charles Marwick, a Scot who lives in Georgetown, Washington, D.C., makes a tasty dish with lamb or veal liver, pinhead oatmeal, suet, minced onions and lamb, and gravy that he has served at New Year's parties. In Albuquerque, New Mexico, Olive and Elizabeth McAskill prepare a haggis flavored with green chiles. A Nova Scotia specialty called *Mareck* is made with beef casings that are stuffed with seasoned oats, onions, and suet, tied up and simmered in water for several hours, then chilled and sliced.

Etta MacKay's favorite vegetarian haggis is made with a mixture of oats, pinhead oatmeal, toasted walnuts, chopped onions, mushrooms, carrots, red kidney beans, garlic, herbs, spices, and a little whisky that is baked in large, whole, unpeeled onions.

The "Shaw Haggis" of Tim and Eileen Shaw Cayler is a hearty combination of beef heart and liver, lamb shoulder, ground elk meat, toasted oatmeal, chopped onions, and beef bouillon seasoned with cayenne pepper, ground nutmeg, rosemary, ginger, paprika, ground cloves, salt, and pepper. It is bumped up "right sharply with a couple of drams of good single malt." Cooked in a slow cooker, it is served garnished with sprigs of boxwood—and with pride.

A popular menu item at a recent Smithsonian Folklife Festival in Washington, D.C., was a haggis burger served with crisps (fried potatoes).

Many Scottish Americans purchase haggis in cans and at specialty food stores selling Scottish products. A Kansas City, Missouri firm called Scotsfare sells haggis pups, small sausages made of lean pork and seasonings, and larger kinds of haggis.

Jim Walters, a Texan of Scottish descent who admits to liking haggis after first tasting it on a trip to Scotland, resolved to make it himself. After a great many attempts, he devised an authentic-tasting mixture of beef sirloin (from Ohio-raised Scottish Highland cattle), liver, and suet, plus pin oats, onions, pepper, and mace, cooked by a secret process and without the sheep's stomach, that has proved to be a winner. The king of The Caledonia Kitchen, the name of his firm, now sells his favorite food in cans on his Web site and at Scottish festivals in the U.S. His product also won fifth place at a recent *Scotland* magazine haggis taste-off. Walters is a lover of all things Scottish, from food to music and history, and is a member of several associations dedicated to the spreading of Scottish culture.

While served in various forms for many Scottish-American meals and celebrations, haggis is a particular favorite on Hogmanay (New Year's Eve), St. Andrew's Night, and especially Burns Night (January 25), an important event in countries around the world wherever those of Scottish descent live. For the highlight of the traditional meal is, to the skirl of bagpipes, applause, and cry of "Hail, Great Chieftain," the arrival of the haggis on a silver platter. It is then ceremoniously cut with a *skein dhu*, a dirk (short straight dagger worn in the stocking), as everyone joins in a Gaelic toast of *"slainte,"* or "good health." The haggis is served regally with *"neeps an' tatties"* (mashed turnips and potatoes) and many "wee nips" of Scotch whisky.

Since the 19th century, the Illinois St. Andrew's Society has held a "Feast of the Haggis," one of the largest and most important events in the Chicago area and possibly the city's oldest annual ethnic celebration. An elegant banquet rich in traditions of the society and the Scotch haggis, it is an important fundraising event.

Vegetables and Salads

Scottish Americans have long paid homage to a wide variety of vegetables and salads by preparing them in a diverse number of interesting and nourishing dishes. Fortunately, their expertise in making the gifts of the garden into inviting creations has been passed on to modern cooks, who serve them for family meals and entertaining.

In early America, when Scottish immigrants were learning about New World plants, especially beans, corn, and squash, and attempting to cultivate Old World favorites, they were confronted with difficulties as they crossed the country. Nevertheless they learned to appreciate all kinds of plants, roots, and herbs. Some are still eaten raw, some cooked, others in either way. All are rich in vitamins and minerals, particularly iron and calcium, and have a low calorie value.

It is not enough, however, to think of vegetables only as good for us. They are also attractive and delectable, excellent in many roles on our menus.

Although Scottish Americans once had to rely on the fresh vegetables grown in their own particular area and were limited to seasonal choices, they now have a plethora of varieties from around our country. Furthermore, there are excellent frozen and canned vegetables.

It was a notable Scottish American, Thomas Jefferson, the great statesman, diplomat, and philosopher, and our third president, who, among his less acclaimed accomplishments, was also devoted to the production of food, especially vegetables. From an early age and throughout his active life, Jefferson maintained a passionate interest in the improvement of not only his own fare but that of his countrymen. Regardless of how occupied he became with other duties, the Virginian found time to pursue his studies in agriculture and viniculture, experiment with seeds and plants, and increase the variety and goodness of the young nation's resources.

In the gardens and lands of his Virginia hilltop home, Monticello, Jefferson applied himself with the same spirit of scientific inquiry that characterized his other endeavors. In addition to experimenting with such seeds and cuttings as he could procure locally, he succeeded in getting a number of them from other parts of the country and world. From his *Garden Book* we learn that in the spring of 1767 Jefferson planted green peas, asparagus, celery, Spanish onions, lettuce, radishes, broccoli, and cauliflower.

At a time when potatoes were considered primarily a food for animals and tomatoes were thought to be poisonous, Jefferson grew and ate the vegetables. He wrote, "The greatest service which can be rendered any country is, to add an useful plant to its culture."

Another Scottish American and a cousin of Thomas Jefferson, John Randolph, loved to work in his Williamsburg gardens and was the author of the earliest American book on kitchen gardening. In *A Treatise on Gardening by a Citizen of Virginia*, Randolph mentioned many of the favorite vegetables of that time. In addition to those grown by Jefferson, these included artichokes, parsnips, salsify, and turnips. Cucumbers were, in Randolph's opinion, "the most refreshing and delicate of all vegetables." He praised watercress for its "agreeable warm taste" and mint "because it strengthens the mind."

Mary Randolph, also a cousin of Thomas Jefferson and a member of "America's Foremost Family," the Randolphs, published *The Virginia Housewife* in 1824. This was our first regional cookbook, and it helped to shape the future of Southern cooking. She was the first author to devote an entire section of her book to vegetables, and she gave sound advice about choosing, preparing, cooking, and serving many varieties, including native kinds such as squash, pumpkins, lima beans, Jerusalem artichokes, and sweet potatoes.

Especially interesting are the numerous recipes using tomatoes at a time when most Americans shunned them. Mary also prepared another Southern favorite, eggplant, which was then a novelty food. It has been said that "everything that could be picked or captured went into her kitchen to be transferred into something delicious."

Mary's book was acclaimed throughout the South, where it

became a standard household guide for everyday cooking and entertaining. She left us a marvelous culinary handbook and is also remembered as a remarkable and accomplished woman of her time, a great Scottish American.

Included here is a representative collection of Scottish vegetable and salad recipes.

Greens

Like their forefathers, Scottish Americans have long been fond of a wide variety of wild and cultivated greens, even those commonly thought of as weeds, such as the dandelion. They pride themselves in making all sorts of greens into delicious, highly nutritious, and attractive dishes.

Southerners became particularly fond of greens such as collards and kale, stalwarts of the cabbage family. These are inexpensive, rich in calcium and vitamin A, and low in calories.

Kale—or *kail,* as the Scots spell it—is a highly esteemed green in Scotland, where the word came to mean all vegetables, as a *kailyard* was actually a vegetable garden. Ubiquitous kale became a primary ingredient in a number of nourishing, simple dishes, such as Kail Brose, originally a pottage of oatmeal, boiling water or milk, and kale. A pudding called Tartan Purry is made with kale and oatmeal. Both the plant and the dishes were introduced to America by Scottish settlers, and they have long been fundamental to home cooking. Cooks understand that kale has an appealing unique texture, firm but not tough, and a refreshing mild flavor. While Scots favor the combination of oats and kale, to which bacon or beef is sometimes added, the vegetable is generally boiled and seasoned with butter, salt, and pepper or combined with mashed potatoes, onions, and milk.

Following is the recipe for a traditional kale dish.

Kailkenney

½ cup rolled oats
1 lb. small, tender kale, washed
4 tbsp. unsalted butter
½ cup chopped green onions, with some tops
½ cup meat broth or water
Salt and freshly ground black pepper, to
    taste
¼ cup light cream
⅛ tsp. freshly grated nutmeg

In a small skillet, toast oats, stirring often, over medium-high heat for 3 minutes, until lightly brown. Remove from the heat; set aside.

Strip kale leaves from stems. Cut leaves into fine slivers. In a large saucepan over medium-high heat, melt 2 tbsp. butter. Add green onions; sauté for 2 minutes. Add kale and broth or water. Season with salt and pepper. Bring to a boil. Reduce heat to medium low. Cook, covered, for 12 minutes, until kale is just tender. Add cream, nutmeg, remaining butter, and oats. Mix well. Cook for 2 minutes. Serve at once with oatcakes or as a side dish. Serves 4.

Potatoes

The versatile potato, native to South America, was introduced to Scotland in the 17th century, where it took some time to be accepted as a food. But over the years, the humble vegetable became a highly prized ingredient in a variety of dishes, including soups, pancakes, breads, and casseroles. Many of them are flavored with herbs, milk, butter, cheese, and oats.

How the American white potato became known as the Irish potato is a bonnie tale. Scotch Irish from Argyle in Scotland who settled Londonderry, New Hampshire, now Derry, introduced the plant and culture of the potato. Until their arrival, the valuable vegetable, if not wholly unknown, was not cultivated in New England. According to historical records, the immigrants planted the first potato on the American continent in 1719, and it came to be generally called the Irish potato, to distinguish the white potato from the sweet potato. On the day of the planting, the local residents celebrated with a Potato Festival.

Be that as it may, as a Scottish American from New Hampshire, I share the opinion that the vegetable should have been called a Scotch or Celtic potato. Alas, it's too late now to change this name.

Given below are some Scottish-American potato recipes.

Prince Edward Island's Baked Potato

Canada's smallest province, Prince Edward Island (P.E.I.) in the Gulf of St. Lawrence, known around the world as the setting of *Anne of Green Gables,* is where Highland Scots settled in the 18th century. It remains Scottish culturally, being home to the MacNeil, MacDonald, and Montgomery families, among others, who enjoy the excellent local foods, including fish and shellfish. "Lobster Suppers" are an institution and usually include baked potatoes or salad. For the island's red acidic soil is excellent for growing root vegetables, chief among them the potato, an important local food and cash crop.

One of the most popular specialties on P.E.I. is the baked potato served with a variety of toppings and enjoyed as a nutritious snack or accompaniment.

4 medium baking potatoes, scrubbed and
  dried
Vegetable oil
1 cup cottage cheese or sour cream
2 tbsp. minced chives
2 tbsp. minced fresh dill or parsley
Salt, to taste

Rub potatoes with oil. With a fork, puncture the skins in several places. In a preheated 425-degree oven, bake potatoes for about 50 minutes, until tender when pierced with a fork. Remove from oven. Make a crosswise cut in the top of each potato and pinch potatoes to let the steam escape.

Meanwhile, in a small bowl, combine cottage cheese or sour cream, chives, and dill or parsley. Season with salt. Spoon over baked potatoes. Serve at once. Serves 4.

Idaho Stuffed Potatoes

One of the world's greatest white potatoes is the large one grown in the volcanic soil of southern Idaho and named for the state. It is highly prized for baking and excellent for stuffing, a favorite preparation of Scottish Americans.

The Scottish American Society of Idaho celebrates the Treasure Valley Highland Games and Celtic Festival in Boise on the third weekend in September.

4 medium Idaho potatoes, scrubbed and
dried
3 tbsp. minced green onions
3 tbsp. minced green peppers
3 tbsp. milk
3 tbsp. unsalted butter
¼ cup grated yellow cheese
Salt and freshly ground black pepper, to
taste

With a fork, puncture potato skins in several places. In a preheated 425-degree oven, bake potatoes for about 50 minutes, until tender when pierced with a fork. Remove from oven. Make a crosswise cut in the top of each potato. Scoop out the insides while still hot, being careful not to break the rest of the skins. In a medium bowl, mash potatoes well. Add green onions and peppers, milk, 2 tbsp. butter, and cheese. Season with salt and pepper. Spoon into potato shells. Dot tops with remaining butter. Return to oven; bake 15 minutes longer. Serve at once. Serves 4.

Rumbledethumps

Certain Scottish dishes attract considerable attention because of their name as well as their taste. This subtle blend from Scotland's Borders region of boiled cabbage, mashed potatoes, butter, and chives, served as a meatless entrée or accompaniment, is one of them. Rumbled means "mixed" and thumped "bashed together," hence the unusual name.

At the Scottish Lion Inn, North Conway, New Hampshire, this Borders specialty developed such a following that, according to a spokesperson, hardly a meal is served at there without it.

The annual New Hampshire Highland Games, the largest Scottish cultural festival in the Northeast, are held at Loon Mountain in Lincoln in late September.

Here is my favorite recipe for this cabbage-potato dish.

1 lb. (about 4 medium) potatoes, peeled and
   cut into small cubes
Salt, to taste
½ cup milk
3 tbsp. unsalted butter
Freshly ground black pepper, to taste
1 lb. (about ½ head) cabbage, shredded
1 medium yellow onion, minced
3 tbsp. chopped chives or parsley
½ cup grated sharp Cheddar cheese

Put the potato cubes with boiling salted water to cover in a medium saucepan over medium-low heat. Cook, covered, for 15 minutes, until potatoes are tender. With a slotted spoon, transfer potatoes to a large bowl; mash. Reserve the liquid in the saucepan. Add milk and 2 tbsp. butter to mashed potatoes. Season with salt and pepper. Mix well. Add cabbage to the reserved potato liquid in the saucepan. Cook over medium-high heat for about 7 minutes, until tender but crisp. Transfer cabbage to potato mixture. Mix well.

Melt remaining butter in a small skillet over medium-high heat. Add onion; sauté until tender, 4 minutes. Add to vegetables. Mix in chives or parsley. Spoon into a shallow baking dish. Sprinkle the top with cheese. Brown under a hot broiler until cheese melts and the top is golden. Or bake in a preheated 450-degree oven for 12 minutes. Serves 4 to 6.

Stovies

This traditional Scots specialty was introduced to America by the early settlers and is still a favorite dish. The word stovies comes from the French *étouffer*—to cook slowly in an enclosed pot. The dish is also called *stoved* potatoes. Some cooks prepare it with sliced potatoes; others leave them whole and add leftover cooked meat and a little gravy.

½ cup rolled oats
2 tbsp. bacon drippings or unsalted butter
1 large yellow onion, quartered and thinly
    sliced
2 lb. (about 10) small new potatoes, peeled
½ cup meat broth or water
Salt and freshly ground black pepper, to
    taste

In a small, dry skillet, toast oats, stirring often, over medium-high heat for 3 minutes, until lightly brown. Remove from the heat; set aside.

In a large saucepan, heat drippings or melt butter over medium-high heat. Add onion; sauté until tender, 4 minutes. Add potatoes and broth or water. Season with salt and pepper. Reduce heat to medium low. Cook, covered, for about 25 minutes, until potatoes are just tender. Sprinkle with oats. Cook for another 5 minutes. Serve at once. Serves 6.

Picnic Potato Salad

Potato salad holds a place of honor at picnics. It is greatly favored by Scottish Americans for summer outdoor meals and Games and Gatherings, where cooks often vie with each to offer original and praiseworthy specialties.

The potatoes used in salad should be of top quality and freshly cooked. The best kinds are the waxy ones, such as small or medium reds, or long whites that have a low starch content and firm texture. They will remain firm when cut after cooking, will not become mushy in the salad, and will not absorb too much dressing.

6 medium waxy potatoes, washed
Salt, to taste
Juice of 2 large lemons
1 cup diced celery
¾ cup peeled, seeded, and diced cucumber
⅓ cup diced green pepper
⅓ cup chopped fresh parsley
Freshly ground black pepper, to taste
About ¾ cup mayonnaise

In a medium saucepan, cook potatoes, covered with salted boiling water, over medium-high heat for 25 minutes, until tender. Drain; peel. While potatoes are still warm, cut into 1-inch cubes. Put in a bowl; add lemon juice; mix well. Leave at room temperature for 30 minutes. Add celery, cucumber, green pepper, and parsley. Season with salt and pepper. Mix well. Add enough mayonnaise to bind ingredients. Refrigerate or serve. Serves 6 to 8.

Candied Sweet Potatoes

Since colonial times, sweet potatoes, botanical cousins of the morning glory and native to South America, have been popular in the South, where Scottish Americans learned to cook and like them. In his letters, George Washington referred to the sweet potato as the common or country potato. The vegetables have a high food value, are a rich source of vitamin A, and have worthwhile quantities of vitamin C. Early Scots liked to roast them in hot ashes, an old Southern custom, or broil them on a griddle.

Here is one typical recipe.

6 medium sweet potatoes, scrubbed
Salt, to taste
¾ cup brown sugar
⅓ cup unsalted butter

In a medium saucepan, cook potatoes, covered with salted boiling water, over medium-high heat for 30 minutes, until just tender. Cool, peel, and slice. Arrange in layers in a buttered shallow baking dish, sprinkling each layer with salt, brown sugar, and bits of butter. In a preheated 350-degree oven, bake for 30 minutes. Serve at once. Serves 6.

Note: This dish may also be made with honey and orange juice.

Baked Rutabaga and Apples

Scots have long been fond of root vegetables, especially the turnip, which can be prepared in a number of appetizing dishes. Neep Purry is a ginger-flavored puree, an old-time favorite. In Scotland the preferred turnip is usually the rutabaga, or yellow turnip, which has an appealing sweet yellow flesh and is generally cooked and mashed with butter or combined with potatoes.

This recipe includes two favorite Scottish foods, rutabaga and apples.

1 rutabaga, about 1¼ lb., washed and peeled
Salt, to taste
3 tart apples, cored and sliced (unpeeled)
¼ cup light brown sugar
2 tbsp. lemon juice
2 tbsp. unsalted butter

Slice rutabaga. In a medium saucepan, cook in salted boiling water to cover over medium-high heat for 10 minutes, until almost tender. Drain. In a shallow baking dish, arrange rutabaga and apple slices in alternating layers, sprinkling each layer with sugar and lemon juice. Dot the top with butter. In a preheated 350-degree oven, bake for 30 minutes, until rutabaga and apple slices are tender. Serves 4 to 6.

New Brunswick Seaweed

Dulse, the name for an edible seaweed that grows in profusion on the rocky shores of Grand Manan Island, New Brunswick, Canada, ten miles from the coast of Maine, is a sought-after delicacy long treasured by northeastern Scottish Americans. It is also gathered off the shores of Nova Scotia.

Fresh, thickly crumpled dulse is reddish brown in color, rubbery in texture, and briny in taste. A good source of protein, iron, iodine, zinc, copper, and other minerals, it is also sold in dried, powdered, or flaked form in some groceries and health-food stores. Some say this seaweed is an acquired taste.

Dulse is eaten in sandwiches, raw or (usually) dried. When fried, it is enjoyed as a snack, like potato chips. It is also used to enhance soups, chowders, seafood, or vegetable dishes, especially potato, or to make a pungent tea or other drinks.

Poor Man's Asparagus

In early America, scallions, also known as green or spring onions, were nicknamed "Poor Man's Asparagus," as they were more available and less expensive than the real thing. This appealed to thrifty Scots. The onions are sweet and mild, and their tops may also be eaten.

4 bunches green onions
2 tbsp. unsalted butter
2 tbsp. all-purpose flour
1 cup light cream or milk
Salt and freshly ground black pepper, to
**   taste**
2 egg yolks
Dash of grated nutmeg
4 slices toast (optional)

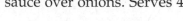

Trim onions, cutting off roots and any wilted tops, leaving about 2 inches of green. Wash onions well. In a covered medium skillet over medium-low heat, cook in a little water to cover for 10 minutes.

Meanwhile, in a medium saucepan, melt butter over medium-low heat. Stir in flour. Gradually add cream or milk. Cook slowly, stirring, until thickened and smooth. Season with salt and pepper.

In a small dish, mix egg yolks with a little of the hot sauce. Return to the saucepan. Cook until thickened and smooth. Add nutmeg. Place hot onions on toast, if desired. Spoon sauce over onions. Serves 4.

Alexander Livingston's Tomato Salad

Reynoldsburg, Ohio, on the outskirts of Columbus, has an annual Tomato Festival in September in recognition of the town's most famous native, Alexander W. Livingston, and his vast accomplishments in agriculture. He was internationally renowned as a horticulturist and as one of the most important developers of tomato varieties in America during the late 19th century. Reynoldsburg claims to be the home of the commercial tomato. The festival features booths selling tomato fudge, jellies, cakes, pies, and breads as well as contests for tomatoes of all sizes.

Livingston and the Tomato by A. W. Livingston, about the author's tomato experiences, was published in 1893 and is now available as a reprint with a new foreword. It was the first comprehensive book published about tomatoes in America and features tomato recipes and helpful data about canning and making soups.

This salad is typical of those enjoyed by Scottish Americans in Ohio.

**4 large ripe tomatoes, peeled and thickly
  sliced
1 bunch green onions, cleaned, sliced with
  1½-inch green tops
¼ cup olive oil
1½ tbsp. cider vinegar
1 tsp. sugar
Salt and freshly ground pepper, to taste**

Arrange tomato slices, overlapping, in a shallow serving dish. Sprinkle with green onions. Combine oil, vinegar, and sugar. Season with salt and pepper. Mix well. Pour over tomatoes. Let stand at room temperature for several minutes, or serve at once. Serves 6.

Skirlie Tomatoes

Skirlie, or skirl-in-the-pan, is an old Scots oatmeal stuffing that has an appealing nutty flavor. The name comes from the frizzling sound made by suet or fat frying in a skillet. This is one variation of the recipe.

6 medium ripe tomatoes, peeled
½ cup (1 stick) unsalted butter
2 cups minced yellow onions
2 cups rolled oats
½ cup chopped fresh parsley
Salt and freshly ground black pepper, to
    taste

Cut a thin slice from the top of each tomato; scoop out pulp. Invert tomatoes to drain.

In a large skillet, melt butter over medium-high heat. Add onions; sauté until tender, 4 minutes. Reduce the heat to medium low. Add oats; cook slowly, stirring often, until butter is absorbed, about 10 minutes. Stir in parsley. Season with salt and pepper. Spoon the mixture into tomato shells, dividing evenly. Serve cold or bake in a preheated 375-degree oven 30 minutes. Serves 6.

Fried Green Tomatoes with Milk Gravy

This old-fashioned country dish is a favorite of Scottish Americans living in the South. It's a good accompaniment to fried chicken.

6 medium green tomatoes
About ½ cup all-purpose flour
Salt and freshly ground black pepper, to
    taste
About 5 tbsp. bacon drippings or vegetable
    shortening
1 cup milk

Wash tomatoes; remove stem ends; cut tomatoes into thick slices. Dredge in flour seasoned with salt and pepper. In a heavy skillet, heat 2 tbsp. bacon drippings or shortening over medium-high heat. Quickly sauté tomato slices, a few at a time, until golden brown on both sides. Remove to a hot platter when cooked and keep warm, continuing to sauté and adding drippings or shortening as needed, until all tomatoes are cooked.

Reduce the heat to medium low. Mix 2 tbsp. flour into drippings or shortening, stirring. Gradually add milk. Cook slowly, stirring constantly, until thickened and smooth. Spoon over tomatoes. Serves 4 to 6.

Iowa Corn Salad

Since ancient Indian times, the Midwestern land that is now the state of Iowa has been famous for its golden harvest of corn, which has to be "knee-high by July" if it is to be a bumper crop. All through the 1800s, Scottish settlers arrived there, bringing with them their traditional recipes and learning to enjoy the array of local corn dishes, including salads.

Among the state's notable Scottish-American families are three generations of the Wallace family, farmers, journalists, and authors, who rose to national prominence and shaped America's agricultural policies. Henry A. Wallace was a U.S. secretary of agriculture and vice-president and, in 1948, campaigned for president.

2 cups cooked fresh corn or canned whole-
    kernel corn, drained
¾ cup peeled, seeded, and diced cucumber
½ cup diced green pepper
2 tbsp. grated onion
3 tbsp. cider vinegar
1 tbsp. sugar
2 tsp. celery seed
Salt and freshly ground black pepper, to
    taste

In a medium bowl, combine corn, cucumber, green pepper, and onion.

In a small saucepan over medium-high heat, combine vinegar, sugar, and celery seed. Season with salt and pepper. Bring to a boil. Pour over the vegetables. Cool. Serves 4.

Darien Carrot-Peanut Salad

The coastal community of Darien, Georgia, was settled by Scottish Highlanders who arrived in 1735 and became known for their strong sense of family, integrity, and proud work ethic. By the 1800s, the Gaelic-speaking colony, despite hardships and challenges, was a prosperous trade and shipping center and figured prominently in Georgia's history. In the center of Darien, the Highlander Monument, ornamented with the Scottish thistle and the Georgia Cherokee rose, bears a bronze panel depicting a group of Scottish Highlanders. Part of the inscription reads: *Their ideals, traditions, and culture enriched the land of their adoption.*

In Georgia, a favorite salad is made with grated carrots, peanuts, and raisins.

3 cups peeled, grated carrots
1 cup chopped peanuts
½ cup seedless raisins
1 cup mayonnaise
3 tbsp. orange juice
6 navel orange slices
6 crisp lettuce leaves, washed and dried

In a large bowl, combine carrots, peanuts, raisins, mayonnaise, and orange juice. Refrigerate, covered with plastic wrap, for 1 hour or longer to blend flavors. When ready to serve, place each orange slice on a lettuce leaf on an individual serving plate. Top each orange slice with a mound of carrot mixture. Serves 6.

Appalachian Buttermilk Slaw

During the 1700s, a steady influx of immigrants from Northern Ireland and Scotland, looking for land to farm and the right to preserve their simple ways, settled in Southern Appalachia, the future Virginia, Tennessee, Carolinas, and beyond. Today their Scotch-Irish descendants are still there and celebrate their heritage with Games and Gatherings.

A favorite staple food, cabbage, is enjoyed in a number of salads, including those called slaw, coleslaw, or wilted slaw. Generally featuring shredded green cabbage, these are often moistened with a buttermilk dressing.

¼ **cup buttermilk**
¼ **cup sour cream**
1 tbsp. cider vinegar
1 tbsp. sugar
1 tsp. celery seed
Salt and freshly ground black pepper, to
   taste
3 cups finely shredded green cabbage (1
   small head), firmly packed
¼ **cup minced red or white onions**
½ **cup minced carrots**
¼ **cup minced fresh parsley**

In a small bowl, whisk together buttermilk, sour cream, vinegar, sugar, and celery seed. Season with salt and pepper. In a medium bowl, combine cabbage, onions, carrots, and parsley. Add buttermilk mixture. Refrigerate. Toss before serving. Serves 6.

Hawaiian Fruit Salad

The Scottish connection to Hawaii reaches back to Capt. James Cook, born in Yorkshire to Scottish parents, who came upon the archipelago in 1778. Since then, many Scots, including political counselors and agriculturists or "scientific gardeners," have played a significant role in Hawaiian history. A Scot, Robert Wylie, was foreign minister there. A Scottish family, the Sinclairs, acquired the small island of Niihau, which their descendants still own. Those who worked as sugar technicians and plantation overseers added their special touch to Hawaiian menus with scones and shortbread, and Scots became fond of local island foods, including luscious fruit.

The annual Hawaiian Scottish Festival & Games are held in Honolulu in April.

4 ripe or preserved kumquats, sliced
2 cups chopped fresh or canned pineapple
1 cup halved orange sections, peeled and
** membranes removed**
½ cup mayonnaise
2 tbsp. pineapple or orange juice
¼ tsp. ground ginger
Salt, to taste
Crisp lettuce leaves, washed and dried
2 tbsp. chopped macadamia nuts or almond
** slivers**

In a medium bowl, combine kumquats, pineapple, and oranges. Mix mayonnaise, pineapple or orange juice, ginger, and salt. Just before serving, add to the fruit. Serve in lettuce cups and sprinkle with nuts. Serves 4.

Salmagundi

An old English hearty salad with the fascinating name of salmagundi, sallad magundy, solomon grundy, or other variations, meaning a mixture, was a favorite early American specialty. Mary Randolph gives directions for making "salmagundi" in a section called "Little Dishes for a Second Course or Supper" in *The Virginia Housewife*.

By the early 1800s, salmagundi had become a part of the American parlance. Washington Irving, a distinguished Scottish-American author, the son of an Orcadian fisherman (the Orkney Islands of Scotland), and recognized as "America's first great man of letters," contributed a series of genial and humorous essays to a periodical called *The Salmagundi Papers*, and a social and dining club named after the dish was formed in 1871.

Prepared in several variations, the salad is made with colorful ingredients artfully arranged on a bed of greens. Serve it for a weekend luncheon or supper.

1 cup olive oil
⅓ cup red-wine or tarragon vinegar
2 to 3 tsp. sugar
½ tsp. dry mustard
¼ tsp. paprika
2 tsp. prepared horseradish
Salt and freshly ground black pepper, to
  taste
2 qt. salad greens (Boston, romaine, leafy
  lettuce), washed, dried, torn into bite-size
  pieces, and chilled
1 bunch watercress, cleaned, washed, and
  dried
1 lb. cooked white meat of chicken or
  turkey, ham, or beef, julienned
¾ lb. yellow cheese, julienned
4 hard-cooked eggs, shelled and sliced

6 gherkins, cut in halves
1 can (2 oz.) flat anchovies, drained and
  chopped
8 pitted black olives

In a small bowl or jar, combine oil, vinegar, sugar, mustard, paprika, and horseradish. Season with salt and pepper. Refrigerate.

When ready to serve, arrange greens and watercress to form a mound or pyramid in the center of a salad bowl. Surround with strips of meat, with sprinkles of cheese placed between them. Garnish with eggs, gherkins, anchovies, and olives to make an attractive salad. Shake dressing and serve with the salad. Prepare salad beforehand and refrigerate until ready to serve, if desired. Serves 8.

Barley, Oats, and Cornmeal

Fruits of the field, as cereals and grain are sometimes called, have been favorite Scottish foods for so long that their culinary versatility is not always appreciated. In recent years, our menus have included more creations made with barley, oats, and cornmeal as cooks have devised more interesting dishes featuring them.

Scottish Americans brought their fondness for barley, an ancient nutritious grain, from their homeland, where it was an important crop. It was commonly used to make the daily bread, including bannocks and scones, and classic soups, especially Scotch Broth. Barley was vital to the production of Scotch whisky, and barley water was a common medicinal drink.

Scots are fond of barley porridge, once a staple breakfast dish that in America can be made with whole hulled barley, sometimes called Scotch barley. It is sold in health and specialty food stores. Darker in color, nuttier, and chewier than pearl barley, it is the most nutritious form of this grain, as it still has its bran coating. Cooked barley has an appealing chewy texture and assertive flavor.

Oats, the "flower of Scottish soil," have sustained Scots for centuries. Oats are the most nutritious of grains and an excellent energy food, containing B and E vitamins and nine minerals. They have the highest level of protein of any grain and are naturally low in sodium, sugar, and cholesterol. Oats have a sweet, nutty flavor and crunchy texture and are an excellent cooking and baking ingredient. "Oatmeal cakes and oatmeal porridge have made Scotchmen" is a favorite saying.

In early times, oats became the primary source of sustenance for the Scots. Through necessity, cooks created the most practical and imaginative of all the world's oat dishes. An old Scottish cookbook stated quite correctly that the oat is "one of the sweetest grains to cook with."

It has been recorded that oats were brought on a British ship in the 1600s to Massachusetts, where they were planted and became a staple food in the daily diet. But for a long time they failed to yield plentiful crops, as did wheat and corn.

Eventually, however, the grain became an important crop in some Midwestern states and in Western Canada.

Over the years, Scottish Americans used oats in making soups, vegetable and meat dishes, seafood specialties, puddings, desserts, a wide range of baked goods, and drinks, as well as the traditional porridge and haggis.

Oats are a whole grain. Hulled oats (or groats, as they are called) still contain their original bran, germ, and endosperm. In the United States, the most common form of oats are rolled, so called because the whole groats are steamed and then flattened between rollers into flakes. The two more widely available are the gray-white regular (also called old-fashioned) and quick. Both have the same nutritional benefits. They can be used interchangeably in most recipes.

Scotch oats are cut with stone rather than steel rollers and are nuttier, chewier, and more coarsely ground. Sold in specialty or health-food stores, they take longer to cook.

When Scots mention oatmeal, they mean the milled grain. They use fine, medium, and coarse oatmeal for several dishes. In America, oats are popularly called oatmeal, a catchall term for various kinds of oats and popular breakfast cereals such as porridge.

In the 1980s, many health professionals touted oat bran, the outer covering of the grain, as a miracle food. It is rich in water-soluble fiber that is believed to help lower cholesterol levels for many persons when used as a part of a total dietary program. Several Scottish recipes include the oat bran.

Early Scottish Americans quickly discovered that their fate in the New World depended on corn, and from the Indians they learned how to pound dried corn kernels in stone or wooden mortars. Later, Scots in new settlements built grist mills, turned by water, to grind corn for their daily cornmeal.

For the new immigrants, wheat flour was a luxury, so cornmeal was their only flour for porridges, puddings, breads, and other baked goods. A staple in every colonial home was a simple porridge called cornmeal mush, nothing more than boiled cornmeal topped with milk and sometimes sweetened with maple syrup or honey. In New England, the dish was called hasty pudding, although it was also called stirabout, made in Scotland with oats. During the long, slow cooking, it had to be mixed often. The name "hasty" was applied because it could be served at a moment's notice to hungry children and workers. Leftover cold mush was fried and served with maple syrup or molasses.

Today there are two types of cornmeal. The best is made from whole corn, ground between stones and sold as "stone ground" or "water ground." Because the skin and germ are not removed, this is nutritious but will not keep for long. It is advisable to buy this in small quantities.

"New process" cornmeal is ground between steel rollers after the hull and germ are removed. It is dry and granular, and because of its lower fat content it keeps better. Both kinds are available as either yellow or white cornmeal.

Given below is a collection of delicious barley, oat, and cornmeal recipes.

Barley Porridge with Fruit

This change-of-pace porridge is flavored with fruit and brown sugar.

2½ cups water
Salt, to taste
1 cup hulled barley
1 tbsp. unsalted butter, softened
½ cup raisins
½ cup diced pitted dates
2 tbsp. brown sugar

In a medium, heavy saucepan, bring water to a boil over medium-high heat. Add salt. Gradually add barley, stirring. Reduce the heat to medium low. Cook, covered, stirring occasionally, for about 1 hour, until barley is tender but chewy. Check for doneness during cooking. Remove from heat.

Mix remaining ingredients together. Stir into barley. Serves 4.

Barley-Applesauce Pudding

This is a flavorful baked dish made with two Scottish-American favorite foods that can be served as an accompaniment for meats or poultry or as a dessert.

3 cups cooked hulled barley
½ cup diced pitted dates
½ cup chopped golden raisins
½ cup chopped walnuts
3 tbsp. light brown sugar
½ tsp. ground cinnamon
½ tsp. ground nutmeg
2 cups applesauce
⅓ cup slivered blanched almonds

In a large bowl, combine barley, dates, raisins, walnuts, brown sugar, cinnamon, and nutmeg. Stir in applesauce. Mix well. Spoon into a buttered 1½-qt. round baking dish. Sprinkle the top with almonds. Bake in a preheated 350-degree oven for 30 minutes. Serve hot. Serves 6.

Toasted Oats

Toasting oats gives them a rich, light-brown color; a nutty flavor; and a pleasing, slightly crunchy texture. They can be used in some recipes as a substitute for nuts, providing fewer calories, or for breadcrumbs, offering more nutrition. Add them as extenders to hamburgers or meatloaves. Sprinkle them over cold or hot cereals, salads, cream puddings, or chopped fresh fruit. Here are two methods for toasting oats.

1. Spread 1 cup uncooked rolled (old-fashioned) oats in a medium ungreased skillet. Cook over medium-high heat for about 3 minutes, stirring 2 or 3 times, until the edges are a light golden brown. Remove from heat; cool. Use or store in a tightly covered container in the refrigerator. Makes 1 cup.

2. Spread 1 cup uncooked rolled (old-fashioned) oats on an ungreased baking pan. Bake in a preheated 350-degree oven for about 15 minutes, stirring 1 or 2 times, until the edges are a light golden brown. Remove from oven; cool. Use or store in a tightly covered container in the refrigerator. Makes 1 cup.

Note: To toast oats in the oven in quantity, increase the baking time to 20 or 25 minutes. Cool and store. Toasted oats will keep for up to 3 months in the refrigerator.

Sweet Oat Topping

Here's a flavorful oat topping that is good to serve over hot cereal, chopped fresh fruit, or ice cream or to eat as a snack.

1½ cups rolled oats
½ cup light brown sugar, firmly packed
½ cup chopped walnuts or blanched
   almonds
½ tsp. ground cinnamon
½ cup (1 stick) unsalted butter, melted

In a medium bowl, combine oats, sugar, walnuts or almonds, and cinnamon. Stir in butter. Mix well.

In a small skillet, sauté the oat mixture over medium-high heat, stirring often, for about 5 minutes, until crisp and golden. Remove from heat. Spread the mixture on a baking sheet. Cool. Use or store in a tightly covered container in the refrigerator. Makes about 2 cups.

Crunchy Savory Oat Topping

Serve this topping over soups, salads, cooked vegetables, or baked dishes.

2 cups rolled oats
⅓ cup wheat germ
⅓ cup hulled sunflower seeds
⅓ cup grated Parmesan cheese
1 tsp. dried oregano
½ tsp. dried basil
Salt and freshly ground black pepper, to
    taste
½ cup (1 stick) unsalted butter, melted

In a large bowl, combine oats, wheat germ, sunflower seeds, cheese, oregano, and basil. Season with salt and pepper. Add butter; mix well. Spread the mixture in a large shallow pan. In a preheated 350-degree oven, bake for 15 minutes, stirring once or twice, until light golden brown. Remove from pan; cool. Use or store in a tightly covered container in the refrigerator. Makes about 3⅓ cups.

Porridge

The most famous Scottish dish made from oatmeal is porridge, traditionally and respectfully spoken of as "they." "They're fine, halesome food, they're grand food, parritch," wrote Robert Louis Stevenson in *Kidnapped.*

A steaming bowl of nourishing porridge brings back many a warm feeling for Scottish Americans, who treasure it as their national breakfast dish and beloved morning staple.

"'Tis a dreary morning that doesn't begin with porridge. Enjoy it and ye're off to a good start," my father would proclaim as we prepared for a cold winter or warm summer day. In our household, a bowl of the hot cereal for breakfast was a ritual. It had been prepared the night before, left on the wood-burning black stove to be reheated, and then served with rich milk, honey or brown sugar, or, better still, a drizzle of maple syrup.

"The halesome parritch, Chief of Scotia's food," as Robert Burns, Scotland's national poet, called it, is a delight to prepare and serve and is accompanied by fascinating tradition and ritual. Here are a few tidbits about it.

For porridge oats, use milled (a coarsely ground product) rather than rolled oats that are sold in America as Scotch or Irish oatmeal. Prepare according to package directions. At one time, each Scottish home had a large iron pot called a goblet that was used exclusively for making porridge. Most Scots now use a heavy saucepan. To prepare the porridge properly, bring the water to a rapid bowl and add the oatmeal, letting it fall in a steady stream from your left hand, while with your right hand stirring constantly with a porridge stick called a spurtle. If you don't have a spurtle, use a wooden spoon.

It is essential to thoroughly combine the water and oatmeal to eliminate lumps. Porridge was once called stirabout because it was stirred in a clockwise or "sunwise" direction (following the course of the sun) with the right hand. This is not only convenient but Scots believed that the routine ensured good luck. Salt, added after the porridge has cooked for 10 minutes or longer, is an essential ingredient as it brings out the nutty flavor of the oats.

The Scottish-American ritual of eating porridge is traditionally as serious as its cooking. It begins with spooning the piping-hot cooked porridge into a porringer, a wooden bowl. The common utensil for eating the porridge is a large, round, horn spoon (to avoid burning the mouth). Then each spoonful is dipped into a side dish of cold cream or milk, giving a desirable contrast of hot and cold as it is eaten. Purists maintain that porridge should be eaten without any sweetening, only a pinch or two of salt. But Scots do use honey, golden syrup, or brown sugar. Sprinkling white sugar over the cereal is frowned upon.

Traditionally, porridge was eaten while standing. The reason is not clear. Some Scots say that this way the porridge was more easily digested. Others point out that the custom dates back to the time of the feuding clansmen, when it was advisable to have one's back to the wall. This was thought to be the only safe position for a beleaguered Highlander who feared a stab in the back from a treacherous neighbor. Also, the person could remain alert, ready for a surprise attack or urgent call from the chieftain.

As the Scots say, all you need for a perfect porridge, besides the oats, is some fresh spring water, a little salt (added near the end of the cooking), and, ideally, some Scottish hill or sea air. A true Highlander believed that porridge was eaten "properly" with a dram or two of Scotch whisky.

Porridge need not always be the same traditional dish. The basic preparation can be enhanced with a little butter, some currants or raisins, or chopped or thinly sliced dried fruit (pitted dates and prunes, stemmed figs) added to the porridge just before or after it has finished cooking. For toppings, sprinkle with toasted or uncooked rolled oats, ground cinnamon or nutmeg, fresh berries, sliced fresh fruit, grated or shredded coconut, applesauce, and/or chopped nuts.

Given below are some porridge recipes.

John Muir's Honey Porridge

One of America's most famous naturalists, John Muir, born in 1838 in Dunbar, Scotland, came to the United States when he was 11 years old. The family settled in Wisconsin, where the rugged frontier life inspired in John a love of the outdoors. For years he traveled in America, writing articles about his experiences, inventions, plants, and the environment. In California he assisted his father-in-law in managing a fruit ranch and undertook conservation work. The John Muir Trail is a 212-mile path through California's Sierra Nevada Mountains.

During his childhood, breakfast was "simple oatmeal porridge, usually with a little milk or treacle, served in wooden dishes called 'luggies,' formed of staves hooped together like miniature tubs about four or five inches in diameter," John wrote in his memoir. "We never dreamed of anything to come after the porridge, or asking for more."

This recipe is a favorite porridge of a Muir admirer.

1½ **cups skim milk**
Salt, to taste
⅔ **cup rolled (old-fashioned) oats**
2 tbsp. honey, preferably heather
2 tbsp. cold cream
2 tbsp. toasted rolled oats

In a medium saucepan, combine milk and salt over medium-high heat and bring just to the boiling point. Slowly add oats, stirring constantly. Reduce the heat to medium low. Cook, uncovered, stirring occasionally, for about 3 minutes. Remove from heat. Cover. Let stand for 3 minutes or until of desired consistency. Stir in honey. Serve topped with cream and toasted oats. Serves 2.

Vermont Fried or Baked Porridge

In the late 1800s, a great many Scots immigrated to Barre, Vermont, in the northern half of the state, to work in the granite quarries creating monuments. Regarded as one of the world's finest granite sculptures, the Robert Burns Memorial Statue, with the figure of the poet atop an enormous granite base, was erected in 1899 near Barre's downtown city park by Scottish-American admirers of Burns.

In Barre, oatmeal was so important in the Scots diet that an area where Scottish families lived was called "Oatmeal Flats." Some descendants recall their grandparents telling them, "If you don't eat your oatmeal, you can't have anything else."

In Vermont, Scottish Americans have devised several ways of using leftover cooked porridge for late-breakfast fare or snacks. Here are three suggestions.

1. Shape ²/₃ cup cold cooked oatmeal porridge into an oval patty. Sprinkle each side with 1 tbsp. toasted rolled oats, pressing them into the oatmeal with the back of a spoon. Refrigerate for 1 hour or longer. In a small skillet, greased with melted butter, fry over medium-high heat for 4 minutes on each side, until golden and crisp. Serve topped with maple syrup or a poached egg and with crisp bacon slices. Serves 1.

2. In a medium bowl, combine ¹/₂ cup warm or cold cooked oatmeal porridge, 2 tsp. brown sugar, 1 tbsp. dried black currants or chopped raisins, 1 tbsp. chopped dried apricots, 1 tbsp. chopped walnuts, and 2 tbsp. light cream or milk. Spoon into a 6-oz. custard cup. In a preheated 375-degree oven, bake for 12 to 15 minutes. Serve in the cup. Serves 1.

3. For a laird's special, shape ²/₃ cup cold cooked oatmeal porridge into a 4 x 2-inch rectangle. Sprinkle each side with 1 tbsp. rolled oats, pressing them into the oatmeal with the back of a spoon. Refrigerate for 1 hour or longer. In a small skillet, greased with melted butter, fry over medium-high heat for 4 minutes on each side, until golden and crisp. Serve topped with 1 to 2 tbsp. Scotch whisky, ¹/₄ cup applesauce, and 2 tbsp. Sweet Oat Topping (see index). Serves 1.

Giant MacAskill's Porridge

At a gathering of the MacAskill Sept Society, a favorite topic is the Cape Breton Giant Angus MacAskill, about whom I had known as a child from my mother, his cousin. Stories are told and songs are sung about his legendary strength and remarkable feats, and his name is firmly entrenched in the minds of MacAskills.

Born in 1825 on the Isle of Bernera in Scotland's Outer Hebrides, Angus was 6 when he migrated with his large family to St. Ann's, Cape Breton, where he grew and broadened, often performing extraordinary deeds. News about the muscular power and remarkable size of "St. Ann's Big Boy" reached P. T. Barnum, who took Angus on tour for five years in the mid-1800s. Displayed as a giant, the Scotsman amazed all who saw him. He and Tom Thumb were billed as the world's largest and smallest human beings as they toured much of the United States and Canada and visited England.

One of Angus's weaknesses was that he could not resist a wager where his great strength was involved. In New York, at the age of 38, he was wounded in an unfortunate accident. He was lifting an anchor and was pierced by one of its flukes. His career faded rapidly and Angus returned to St. Ann's, where he started two gristmills and opened a general store until his sudden death later that same year.

The Giant MacAskill Museum, operated by the Giant MacAskill Heirs Association in Englishtown, is dedicated to the memory of the 7-foot, 9-inch, 425-pound Scot, once the "strongest man on earth." Many of his personal belongings are on display and he is remembered as a "successful public man, who did not feel bigger than he was." And in Dunvegan on the Isle of Skye, there is a one-room thatched Giant Angus MacAskill Museum with a life-size model of the great man and data about his career and times.

Not much is known about the giant's diet except that he ate a large bowl of crowdie (oatmeal and cream) after each meal, and as one MacAskill descendant explained, he was just like any other "braw Scotch laddie" brought up on a Cape Breton diet of dishes made with oats, especially porridge.

Here is a MacAskill porridge recipe, using Scotch oats.

4 cups cold water
⅔ cup Scotch oats
Salt, to taste

In a medium saucepan, bring water to a rapid bowl over medium-high heat. Gradually add oats, stirring with a wooden spoon. Stir until the mixture returns to a boil. Reduce the heat to medium low. Cook, covered, for about 30 minutes, stirring frequently, until it is a desirable thickness. Add salt during the last few minutes of cooking. Serve with milk or cream and, if desired, brown sugar. Serves 4.

Peace River Granola

The Peace River countryside of British Columbia in Canada is famous for its superb grains, including oats. This is a variation of the region's granola recipe.

1½ cups rolled oats
½ cup wheat bran
½ cup wheat germ
½ cup hulled sunflower seeds
½ cup shredded coconut
½ cup chopped walnuts
⅓ cup peanut oil
⅓ cup honey
½ cup chopped raisins

Spread oats in a large shallow pan. In a preheated 350-degree oven, toast oats for 15 minutes, stirring once or twice. Remove from oven but keep oven on. Cool oats.

In a large bowl, combine oats, wheat bran and germ, sunflower seeds, coconut, and walnuts. Mix well.

In a small saucepan, heat oil and honey over medium-high heat. Add to the oat mixture. Mix well. Spread the mixture in a large shallow pan. In the preheated oven, bake for 30 minutes, stirring occasionally, until golden brown. Remove from oven. Cool. Break up the cooled mixture and add raisins. Eat as a snack or with milk as a cold cereal. Or store in a tightly covered container in the refrigerator. Makes 5 cups.

James Polk's Hushpuppies

James Knox Polk, the 11th U.S. president, was a member of a notable Scots-Irish family that first settled in the Chesapeake area of Maryland before moving west to other areas, including Tennessee. He was only 49 when he took office, and he founded the U.S. Naval Academy, authorized the Smithsonian Institution, and created the Department of Interior. James and his wife, Sarah, gave the first Thanksgiving dinner at the White House.

It has been said that James Polk was fond of cornmeal dishes, including one that was commonly called hushpuppies, considered a delicacy of Southern cooking. It became a favorite of many Scottish Americans.

1 cup stone-ground white cornmeal
1 tsp. baking powder
¾ tsp. sugar
½ tsp. salt
1 egg
½ cup milk
3 tbsp. minced onion
Vegetable oil or fat, for frying

In a large bowl, combine cornmeal, baking powder, sugar, and salt. In a small bowl, combine egg and milk, mixing well. Stir into the cornmeal mixture. Add onion; mix well. Drop by tablespoons or small ovals into hot oil or fat (375 degrees) in a deep-fat fryer, turning once or twice, until golden. Drain on paper towels. Makes about 16.

Kentucky Corn Cakes

Originally a part of Virginia Territory, "a new Country Called Kentucky" was, according to one writer, "reckon'd the finest Country in the World, affording almost all the necessities of life Spontaneously." A great many Scots and Scotch Irish, including Daniel Boone, Gen. George Rogers Clark, the founder of Louisville, and William Clark, who established Paducah, became prominent citizens of the state.

The Glasgow Highland Games, an annual "Gathering of Family and Scottish Heritage Celebration" held at Barren River Lake State Resort Park in Lucas, Kentucky, is celebrated in late May with a Torch Light *Ceilidh*, A Festival of Scottish Songs, and a Kentucky Barbecue. 'Tis one of the country's liveliest Scottish Gatherings.

These small corn cakes are sometimes called "batty cakes" or "lacy-edged cakes," as the cooked thin battercakes (pancakes) have crisp edges. They are favorite breakfast fare.

1 cup white cornmeal
½ tsp. baking soda
½ tsp. salt
1 egg
1¼ cups buttermilk

In a medium bowl, combine cornmeal, soda, and salt. In a small bowl, mix egg and buttermilk. Combine mixtures. Beat until smooth. Drop the batter by tablespoons into a greased skillet over medium-high heat, allowing about 2 inches between cakes so they can spread while cooking. Cook until the undersides are golden. Turn and cook on the other sides. Serve at once with syrup, if desired. Serves 4.

Grits

Hominy or hulled corn, prepared generally from kernels of white corn, was once a popular Southern food, commonly served as a whole grain or ground into grits. The finely ground white hominy from the inner white corn and coarser yellow grits are often eaten as a simple porridge. Any leftover cooked grits can be fried or used to make other dishes. In several regions, Scottish Americans adopted the custom of serving grits for breakfast as an accompaniment for bacon and eggs.

Charles Parnell, an engineer and native of Edinburgh, Scotland, is the owner of The Old Mill of Guilford, Oak Ridge, North Carolina, which he restored and operates much the way it did when Daniel Dillon began grinding grain for settlers there in 1767. The Old Mill makes and sells a variety of naturally milled or stone-ground flours, cornmeal, and grits, as well as a wide selection of other products.

Hominy grits, a term synonymous with corn grits, are sold packaged as fine, medium, or coarse grinds and as white or yellow. Two fast-cooked varieties are termed quick, ground finer than standard grits, sometimes labeled as old-fashioned grits, and instant. Grits can be combined with milk, eggs, cheese, or seasonings and baked; or made into croquettes, puffs, pancakes, waffles, muffins, fritters, and soufflés; or used in batter bread and spoon pudding.

Here is a basic recipe for cooking grits.

4 cups water
½ tsp. salt, or to taste
1 cup stone-ground hominy grits
2 tbsp. unsalted butter

In a large saucepan, bring water to a brisk boil over medium-high heat. Add salt. Stir in grits. Reduce the heat to medium low. Cook, stirring frequently, for about 35 minutes, until grits are cooked and thickened. Remove from heat. Add butter, stirring until melted. Serve at once. Serves 4.

Dumfries Cheese Grits

Historic Dumfries, the oldest charter town in Virginia, was founded by Scottish merchants and planters and became a prosperous town known for its Stagecoach Inn and tavern built about 1785 by Col. Alexander Henderson. He organized what was probably the first chain of stores in America and his descendants are still residents of the town. When Dumfries celebrated its 250th anniversary, it honored its founding Scottish families with a colorful Heritage Fair sponsored by the Clan Henderson Society.

Cheese grits made with various flavorings is a favorite Dumfries dish.

4 cups water
½ tsp. salt, or to taste
1 cup stone-ground grits
2 tbsp. unsalted butter
1 cup shredded Cheddar cheese
2 tbsp. brown sugar
Pinch of cayenne pepper, or to taste
¼ tsp. ground white pepper

In a large saucepan, bring water to a brisk boil over medium-high heat. Add salt. Stir in grits. Reduce the heat to medium low. Cook, stirring frequently, for about 35 minutes, until grits are cooked and thickened. Remove from heat. Add butter and cheese, stirring until melted. Stir in sugar and cayenne and white peppers. Mix until smooth. Serve at once. Serves 4.

Breads

Ever since Scots arrived in America, they have been known for their homemade breads, especially bannocks, oatcakes, and scones. The art of baking has long been the glory of the Scottish kitchen. "Every Scotswoman is born with a rolling pin under her arm," proclaimed an early food writer. Making breads is still important in the Scottish-American home.

Bread, a universal food made of flour or meal mixed with a liquid and usually a leavening agent, formed into various shapes, and baked or sometimes fried, comes in hundreds of varieties that are treasured staples for every meal.

Early Scottish settlers living in small American communities or moving across the country learned to use New World corn, and then wheat and oats, for their various baked goods. In many pioneer homes, baking was done in the hearth near an open fire, then in brick ovens or wood-burning stoves before the modern oven came into use. It is in baking that Scots' culinary expertise has been most strongly kept alive, even though traditional recipes have often been altered somewhat to conform to the taste of the adopted country.

In the early 1800s, after the roller mill was invented to crush grain quickly and inexpensively between its revolving cylinders, completely removing the outer covering and germ, the era of commercial white bread began and bakeries became common establishments.

It was an eccentric Scottish-American Presbyterian minister, temperance lecturer, and nutritionist named Sylvester Graham (1794-1851) who led a crusade known as "Grahamism" in the mid-1800s to make Americans think about better health. The best food, according to him, was bread made from an unsifted, whole-wheat flour containing the bran of the whole kernel, which came to be called graham flour. Dubbed the "poet of bran bread," Graham, in his *Treatise on Bread and Breadmaking*, implied that bakery goods were adulterated and he promoted home baking. A flat, slightly sweet wafer made with wheat berries called a graham cracker is his best-known legacy, still a popular cookie and ingredient for breads and cakes. A graham-cracker pastry crust is used to make some pies, cakes, and confections.

In *Housekeeping in Old Virginia* (1879), Marian Cabell Tyree had encouraging words for bread-makers. "*Bread.* I would say to housewives, be not daunted by one failure, nor by twenty. Resolve that you *will* have good bread, and never cease striving after this result till you have effected it."

Fortunately, making nutritious Scottish breads today is not a complicated process, and many of them can be prepared in no time at all. Scots in the South and in eastern Canada introduced several of their traditional breads such as scones, predecessors to biscuits, and griddlecakes, better known as pancakes, and through generations of baking in the home, the appeal of old-time, high-quality products, made with respect for tradition, has persisted.

Bannocks

Typical Scottish bread originated as an unleavened round, flat cake that was cooked on a bakestone and later on a "girdle," or griddle, one of world's oldest cooking utensils, which was brought to Scotland by the early Celts. The bread was called bannock, a word that comes from the Gaelic *bonnach*, meaning cake. Over the years other breads, some soft and quite thick and baked in the oven, would be called bannocks.

In America, pioneers of Scottish descent introduced the bannock, made initially with oats and cooked on a griddle. It has been said that in the South the griddle and oatmeal warmed the heart of the Scot. In many homes, the housewife placed her bannock cakes on a board before glowing coals or on a circular plate of iron suspended over the fire, replaced later by the iron skillet or oven. Like many early recipes, there were adaptations of the original breads from Scotland, with the American versions varying considerably as to ingredients and methods of cooking. One called Indian Bannock, a 19th-century New England bread, was made with cornmeal, sour milk, beaten eggs, and molasses. The bannock became a favorite bread of frontiersmen, campers, and backpackers, as the dry ingredients could be carried in a moisture-proof bag to which cold water was added, and the mixture could be cooked easily on an outdoor fire. One bread called Trapper's Bannock was baked on a grill over hot coals.

As in Scotland, many of the early American bannocks had special significance associated with Celtic symbolism or old religious beliefs. A circle escalloped around the edges represented the sun. At one time, each of the four seasons was greeted with its individual bannock for good fortune. Some Americans still make a Yule bannock and a Halloween bannock.

Here are two bannock recipes.

Whole-Wheat Oat Bannock

This is a crunchy bannock that is good plain or toasted.

1¼ cups rolled oats
1 cup whole-wheat flour
3 tbsp. light brown sugar
1 tbsp. baking powder
¾ tsp. salt
¼ cup (½ stick) unsalted butter, chilled and
    diced
1 egg, beaten
About ½ cup milk

Place oats in a blender or food processor. Cover; blend for about 1 minute, stopping occasionally to stir oats, until a fine flour forms. Turn into a large bowl. Add whole wheat flour, sugar, baking powder, and salt. Mix well. With a pastry blender, cut in butter. Make a well in the center of the ingredients. Add egg and milk, enough to make a soft and moist dough, stirring quickly. Gather to form a ball. Place in the center of a lightly floured baking sheet. With floured hands, shape into an 8-inch round loaf about ¹/₂ inch thick. In a preheated 400-degree oven, bake for about 20 minutes, until golden brown and a tester inserted into the center comes out clean. Remove to a wire rack. Serve warm or at room temperature, cut into wedges, with butter and honey. Makes 1 8-inch round loaf.

Bannock Squares

These are good accompaniments for soup.

½ cup (1 stick) unsalted butter, softened
½ cup light brown sugar, firmly packed
1 egg
2 cups all-purpose flour
1 tbsp. baking powder
½ tsp. baking soda
¾ tsp. salt
1 cup rolled oats
1 cup milk

In a large bowl, cream butter and sugar until light and fluffy. Add egg; mix well. In a medium bowl, combine flour, baking powder and soda, and salt. Stir in oats. Add to butter mixture alternately with milk, mixing until well blended. Turn the batter into a greased 13 x 9 x 2-inch rectangular baking pan. In a preheated 375-degree oven, bake for 40 minutes, until golden brown and a tester inserted into the center comes out clean. Remove from oven. Cool in pan for 10 minutes. Cut into squares. Serve warm or cool, plain or with butter and honey. Makes 24 squares.

Oatcakes

If Scottish Americans have a favorite bread, it is the oatcake, a crunchy biscuitlike roundel with a pleasant nutty taste and plain appearance. When Robert Burns called his beloved Scotland the "Land o' Cakes," he meant the humble oatcake. Although the earliest oatcakes were simple mixtures of oatmeal and water that could be made easily and cooked on a griddle for daily sustenance, through generations of baking, many varieties of oatcakes evolved. All are tasty and rewarding to make.

Wherever Scots settled, they made oatcakes that became traditional everyday fare. Some Scottish Americans recall how their grandmothers made the cakes as a ritual with special implements: a wooden spoon or spurtle for stirring, a grooved rolling pin to make a crisscross pattern on the upper side, a long-handled *spathe* to lift the cakes from the board to the griddle, and a banna-rack or toaster on which the cakes were "finished."

Unlike the wafer-thin Highland oatcakes, made with fine oatmeal, a little hot fat and water, plus a pinch of salt, Scottish-American oatcakes also included white flour, a sweetener (usually brown sugar), a leavening agent, and a shortening. In modern times, cooks sometimes add cream or milk, eggs, and even nuts or raisins. The dough is usually cut into small circles or squares but it can be made into triangles. Some of them are cooked on a griddle but most are baked in the oven. While commercial oatcakes are widely available, some cooks still prefer to make them.

Oatcakes are wonderfully versatile. Eaten throughout the day as snacks, they are also enjoyed at all meals. Oatcakes are good with butter and honey or marmalade for breakfast; with soup or cheeses for lunch; and with lemon curd, jam, or marmalade for afternoon tea. A traditional finale for a Scottish dinner is oatcakes and Stilton or Cheddar cheese.

Following is an oatcake recipe.

Mrs. MacLeod's Oatcakes

For many years the most famous oatcakes in Cape Breton, Nova Scotia, were made by Mrs. Allister MacLeod, who, with her husband, ran a popular guesthouse, the Point, at Ingonish. Situated on the Cabot Trail on a spectacular point of land jutting into the Atlantic, the individual cabins near the main house were named Skye, Dunvegan, and Stornoway, reflecting the colorful history of the Clan MacLeod.

The fascinating origins of the Clan MacLeod can be traced to Leod, born about 1200, the son of Olave the Black, King of Man and the Isles. The Clan MacLeod Society, U.S.A., was founded in 1954 and today there are members in all fifty states. It is affiliated with the Associated Clan MacLeod Societies, which has headquarters in Edinburgh.

Here is the recipe for Mrs. MacLeod's oatcakes.

1½ cups rolled oats
1½ cups all-purpose flour
½ cup granulated sugar
½ tsp. baking soda
1 tsp. salt
¾ cup vegetable shortening
About ⅓ cup cold water

In a large bowl, combine oats, flour, sugar, baking soda, and salt. With a pastry blender, cut in shortening until mixture is like fine crumbs. Add sufficient water, stirring, to make a stiff dough. Gather into a large ball. Place on a lightly floured surface. Divide into 2 parts. With a floured rolling pin, roll each part into a sheet and cut each into 16 2-inch squares. Transfer to lightly greased baking sheets. In a preheated 375-degree oven, bake for 15 minutes, until lightly brown and firm. Remove to a wire rack. Makes 32.

Scones

Of all the superb Scottish-American breads, scones are the most popular. Delectable rich and crumbly biscuitlike cakes eaten for breakfast, with afternoon tea, or during the day as snacks, they are now made in many varieties. The origin of the word scone, pronounced *skonn* (to rhyme with "on"), is not clear. It may come from the Gaelic *sgoon* (block) or *sgoon aram* (block of bread). Some Scots believe that the name came from Scone, a parish where Scottish kings were once crowned on the "Stone of Destiny." Nothing about the scone resembles a stone. The bread is very soft and light, made from white or whole-wheat flour, oatmeal, or mashed potatoes. Sweet cream or milk is used for some varieties.

Over the years, bakers have enriched scones with eggs and butter and added such ingredients as sugar, molasses or honey, as well as currants or raisins, dates, cinnamon, ginger, or other spices.

Although scones are cut into various shapes, the traditional biscuit is made in a small triangle or a "farl," cut from a round of dough before baking. Most scones are now baked, but some, called drop scones, are cooked on a griddle or in a heavy skillet almost like pancakes.

Here are several recipes for scones.

Breakfast Whole-Wheat Scones

2 cups whole-wheat flour
2½ tsp. baking powder
¼ tsp. baking soda
1 tbsp. granulated sugar
½ tsp. salt
⅓ cup vegetable shortening
1 egg
⅔ cup buttermilk

Sift flour, baking powder and soda, sugar, and salt into a large bowl. With a pastry blender, cut in shortening until the mixture is like fine crumbs. Combine egg and buttermilk in a small bowl. Add to the dry ingredients. Mix to form a soft dough. Turn out on a lightly floured surface. Shape into 2 rounds, each about 6 inches in diameter and ½ inch thick. Cut each round into 6 triangles. Place on a lightly greased baking sheet about 1 inch apart. In a preheated 400-degree oven, bake for about 15 minutes, until golden and puffed. Remove to a wire rack. Serve the scones warm with butter and marmalade. Makes 12.

Afternoon Tea Scones

These tender, slightly sweet scones are good for afternoon tea. Serve them split, spread with butter and jam, and slathered with whipped cream.

2 cups all-purpose flour
2 tbsp. granulated sugar
4 tsp. baking powder
½ tsp. salt
¼ cup (½ stick) unsalted butter, chilled and
  diced
2 eggs, beaten
About ⅓ cup light cream
Milk, for topping

In a large bowl, combine flour, sugar, baking powder, and salt. With a pastry blender, cut in butter until the mixture is like fine crumbs. Make a well in the center of the dry ingredients. Add eggs and enough cream, stirring, to make a soft and sticky dough. Gather to form a ball. Place on a lightly floured surface. With floured hands, knead gently. Divide the dough into 2 parts. Roll out each part into a 6-inch circle to a ¹/₂-inch thickness. With a floured 2-inch cutter, cut each circle into rounds, leaving as little dough as possible for rerolling. Place on an ungreased baking sheet, about 1 inch apart. Brush tops lightly with milk.

In a preheated 400-degree oven, bake for about 12 minutes, until golden and puffed. Remove to a wire rack. Allow to cool slightly, about 5 minutes. Makes 20.

Raisin-Oat Scones

These small triangle scones have an appealing crisp texture. Serve with afternoon tea or as a snack.

1 cup all-purpose flour
2 tbsp. light brown sugar
1 tbsp. baking powder
½ tsp. salt
1 cup rolled oats
¼ cup (½ stick) unsalted butter, chilled and
  diced
½ cup golden raisins
½ cup milk

In a large bowl, combine flour, sugar, baking powder, and
salt. Stir in oats. With a pastry blender, cut in butter until the
mixture is like fine crumbs. Stir in raisins. Add milk. Stir
quickly to make a soft and sticky dough. Gather into a ball.
Place on a lightly floured surface. With floured hands, knead
gently. Roll into a circle to a ½-inch thickness. With a floured
sharp knife, cut into 12 equal-sized triangles. Place on an
ungreased baking sheet, about 1 inch apart. In a preheated
425-degree oven, bake for about 12 minutes, until golden and
puffed. Remove from oven to a wire rack. Allow to cool
slightly, about 5 minutes. Serve warm. Makes 12.

Dropped Potato Scones

"Drop" or "dropped" scones may be cooked on a griddle or in a heavy skillet almost like pancakes. Prepare these potato scones beforehand and cook just before serving.

1 cup warm mashed potatoes
1 tbsp. melted unsalted butter
½ tsp. salt
1 egg
2 tbsp. buttermilk
⅛ tsp. baking soda
About ½ cup all-purpose flour

In a medium bowl, combine all ingredients, using as much flour as potatoes will take before becoming too dry. The amount varies with the type of potato used. Drop by tablespoons onto a lightly greased hot griddle or a heavy skillet over medium-high heat. Cook for about 5 minutes on each side, until golden and cooked. Makes about 10.

Pancakes

The pancake, a flat cake of batter cooked on a griddle or in a skillet, has long been a Scottish favorite, prepared with various recipes and shapes. In early America, griddlecakes were a staple dish that could be easily made and cooked just about anywhere. Rural households and pioneer wagons moving across the country kept an earthenware pancake jar with a starter that could be replenished as it was used. Scottish Americans became devotees of stacks of hot steaming pancakes served with syrup or other toppings. The cakes were variously called griddlecakes, hotcakes, hoecakes, wheat cakes, flannel cakes, slapjacks, slappers, flapjacks, or stacks of wheat. There are many kinds of batters, thick or thin, and they can be made in every imaginable variation.

Here are a couple of recipes for pancakes.

Scotch Pancakes

These delectable thin pancakes are also called tea pancakes as they are favorites for afternoon tea or dessert.

2 eggs, separated
1 cup milk
2 tbsp. granulated sugar
2 tbsp. unsalted butter, melted
1 cup all-purpose flour
¼ tsp. salt
⅛ tsp. ground allspice
Unsalted butter, for frying

In a medium bowl, whisk egg yolks and milk. Add sugar and butter; mix well. Gradually sift in flour, salt, and allspice, stirring to thoroughly blend the ingredients. In a separate bowl, beat egg whites until stiff. Fold into the batter.

To cook, for each pancake pour about 2 tbsp. batter all at once onto a well-buttered hot griddle or into a 7- or 8-inch skillet over medium-high heat. Cook for about 3 minutes, until bubbles form on the pancake surface and the underside is light golden brown. With a spatula, turn and cook until golden brown on the other side. Slip onto a warm plate and keep warm in a preheated 250-degree oven while cooking the remaining pancakes.

To serve, spread each pancake with a little butter and sprinkle with sugar and, if desired, a little ground cinnamon. Roll up. Serve at once. Makes about 18.

Mississippi Flannel Cakes

A griddlecake, sometimes called flannel cake, is a thick pancake cooked on a hot griddle and eaten for breakfast or supper in Mississippi. Many Scottish Americans came there from the Piedmont regions of the Carolinas and Virginia and saw the potential in the gently rolling fertile lands for farming and establishing towns. The city of Aberdeen was founded by a Scotsman named Robert Gordon. Many Scots who lived on plantations became known for their lavish meals featuring dishes made with homegrown produce and homemade hot breads. As one Scot remarked, "The wildly romantic South of bygone days that took its pitch from Sir Walter Scott's chivalrous romances was easily visible all along the Mississippi River in the ornate residences."

Scottish Highland Games are held annually at Jackson and Biloxi, among other locales.

2 cups all-purpose flour
2 tsp. baking powder
1 tsp. baking soda
2 tsp. sugar
½ tsp. salt
2 eggs, slightly beaten
1½ cups milk
2 tbsp. melted unsalted butter

Sift flour, baking powder and soda, sugar, and salt into a large bowl. Combine eggs, milk, and butter in a small bowl. Add to flour mixture; blend well. Pour ½ cup of the batter into a greased hot skillet over medium-high heat. Cook until golden brown on one side; turn; brown on the other side. Keep warm. Repeat with the remaining batter. Serve hot with butter or syrup. Serves 4 to 6.

Buttermilk-Oaten Bread

Two favorite ingredients for Scottish-American breads are oats and buttermilk. This nutritious raisin-studded loaf can be used to make sandwiches or eaten as a snack.

2 cups all-purpose flour
3 tbsp. light brown sugar
1 tbsp. baking powder
½ tsp. baking soda
½ tsp. salt
1 cup rolled oats
½ cup raisins
2 tbsp. dark molasses
3 tbsp. unsalted butter, melted and cooled
1½ cups buttermilk

In a large bowl, combine flour, sugar, baking powder and soda, and salt. Stir in oats and raisins; mix well. In a small bowl, combine molasses, butter, and buttermilk. Add to the dry ingredients, stirring only until they are just moistened but combined thoroughly. Turn the batter into a greased 9 x 5 x 3-inch loaf pan. In a preheated 350-degree oven, bake for 1 hour, until the loaf is golden brown and a tester inserted into the center comes out clean. Cool in the pan for 10 minutes. Remove from pan. Cool on a wire rack. Makes 1 loaf.

Pumpkin-Walnut Bread

For many Scottish Americans, the gathering of grains, fruits, and vegetables at the beginning of autumn has long been a happy occasion celebrated with feasting and merry-making. It has been aptly called Harvest Home. Harvest suppers featured hearty homemade fare, including breads made with typical New World foods, such as the pumpkin used in this recipe.

2 cups all-purpose flour
2 tsp. baking powder
½ tsp. baking soda
1 tsp. salt
½ tsp. ground nutmeg
1 tsp. ground cinnamon
2 eggs, slightly beaten
½ cup milk
1 cup granulated sugar
1 cup mashed cooked or canned pumpkin
¼ cup melted unsalted butter
1 cup minced walnuts

Sift flour, baking powder and soda, salt, nutmeg, and cinnamon into a medium bowl. Combine eggs, milk, sugar, pumpkin, and butter in a large bowl; mix well. Add the sifted ingredients; mix well. Fold in walnuts. Turn into a greased 9 x 5 x 3-inch loaf pan. In a preheated 350-degree oven, bake for about 35 minutes, until a tester inserted into the center comes out clean. Remove from oven; let rest for 10 minutes. Turn out on a rack; cool. Makes 1 loaf.

Carolina Pecan-Buttermilk Biscuits

It is very likely that American biscuits developed from Scottish scones brought by early settlers to the Carolinas. This is a basic fine-textured and moist biscuit enhanced with the addition of pecans and a touch of nutmeg.

2 cups all-purpose flour
1 tsp. granulated sugar
1 tbsp. baking powder
½ tsp. baking soda
½ tsp. salt
⅛ tsp. freshly grated or ground nutmeg
¼ cup vegetable shortening
½ cup minced pecans
¾ cup cold buttermilk

In a large bowl, combine flour, sugar, baking powder and soda, salt, and nutmeg. With a pastry blender, cut in shortening until the mixture is like fine crumbs. Add pecans. Toss to mix evenly. Add buttermilk, stirring briskly to blend ingredients. Turn out onto a lightly floured surface. Knead gently about 8 times. Pat or roll out into a circle with a ¹/₂-inch thickness. Using a 2-inch floured biscuit cutter, cut into rounds. Place on a lightly greased baking sheet about 1 inch apart. In a preheated 425-degree oven, bake on the middle rack for 12 to 15 minutes, until pale golden and puffed. Remove from oven to a wire rack. Serve warm. Makes about 14.

Aberdeen Softies

Aberdeen, South Dakota is a beautifully wooded city built artificially on dry prairie land. The town was founded by a party surveying for the Milwaukee railroad in 1881 and named for Aberdeen, Scotland, native city of Alexander Mitchell, general manager of the railroad. Other American cities named Aberdeen include those in California, Maryland, Mississippi, North Carolina, and Washington.

Flaky and golden, these soft biscuits are made with buttermilk and a combination of butter and shortening, which makes them very tender. The addition of sugar enhances the flavor and the biscuits brown better with it.

2 cups all-purpose flour
1 tbsp. granulated sugar
1 tbsp. baking powder
1 tsp. baking soda
1 tsp. salt
3 tbsp. unsalted butter, cold and diced
2 tbsp. vegetable shortening
1 egg
About ½ cup buttermilk
2 tbsp. unsalted butter, melted, for topping

Sift flour, sugar, baking powder and soda, and salt into a large bowl. With a pastry blender, cut in cold butter and shortening until the mixture is like fine crumbs. Add egg and buttermilk, just enough to moisten the mixture. With a fork, stir quickly and briskly to make a light and soft dough. Gather into a ball. Turn out on a lightly floured surface. With floured hands, knead gently about 8 times, handling as little as possible. Roll or pat gently into a ¹/₂-inch thickness. With a floured 2¹/₂-inch round biscuit cutter, cut into rounds, leaving as little dough as possible for rerolling. Place on an ungreased baking sheet, about 1 inch apart. Brush with melted butter. In a preheated 450-degree oven, bake for about 12 minutes, until golden and puffed. Remove to a wire rack. Serve warm with butter. Makes 12.

New Brunswick Blueberry Muffins

These nutmeg-flavored muffins are best made with the small, richly colored, tart, wild blueberries that flourish in Canada's picturesque Maritime Province of New Brunswick. Early Scottish settlers ate them fresh in season and sun-dried them for later use in many dishes.

2 cups all-purpose flour
½ cup granulated sugar
4 tsp. baking powder
½ tsp. freshly grated or ground nutmeg
1 tsp. salt
1 egg
¾ cup light cream or milk
1 cup fresh blueberries
4 tbsp. melted unsalted butter, slightly
  cooled

Sift flour (reserving 2 tbsp. to mix with blueberries), sugar, baking powder, nutmeg, and salt into a large bowl. Whisk egg and cream or milk in a small bowl. Add to the dry ingredients, stirring quickly until just moistened. Coat blueberries with remaining flour. Fold into the batter. Stir in butter; mix well. Do not beat. Spoon into 12 greased 2½-inch muffin-pan cups, filling ⅔ full. In a preheated 400-degree oven, bake for about 25 minutes, until light golden on top and a tester inserted into the center comes out clean. Set aside to cool for 5 minutes before removing the muffins from the cups onto a wire rack. Serve warm with butter, honey, or maple syrup, if desired. Makes 12.

Oat-Bran Muffins

This is my favorite recipe for whole-wheat oat muffins. It is made with oat bran, a favorite Scottish-American health food.

1 cup oat bran
¼ cup whole-wheat flour
1 cup rolled oats
2 tsp. baking powder
2 tsp. baking soda
½ tsp. salt
½ cup raisins
2 tbsp. vegetable oil
¼ cup honey
1 egg white
1 cup buttermilk

In a large bowl, combine bran, flour, oats, baking powder and soda, and salt. Stir in raisins. In a small bowl, whisk oil, honey, egg white, and buttermilk. Add to the dry ingredients, stirring until just moistened. Spoon into 12 greased 2½-inch muffin-pan cups, filling ⅔ full. In a preheated 425-degree oven, bake for 15 to 17 minutes, until golden brown and a tester inserted into the center comes out clean. Set aside to cool for 5 minutes before removing the muffins from the cups onto a wire rack. Serve warm or cool. Makes 12.

William Clark's Cornbread

William Clark, a redheaded Virginian with Scottish ancestors on both sides of his family, was the brother of frontiersman George Rogers Clark and commanded the extraordinary Lewis and Clark expedition of 1804-6. The 28-month, nearly 8,000-mile journey followed the Missouri and Columbia rivers to the Pacific, giving the world its first clear picture of the American West. The daily quest for food was of utmost concern, and Clark's journals recorded what they tasted and enjoyed along the way. It has been said that Clark was very fond of corn and cornmeal bread similar to one made with this typical Virginia recipe.

2 tbsp. unsalted butter
2 cups yellow cornmeal
4 tsp. baking powder
1½ tsp. salt
1 egg
1½ cups milk

Put butter into an 8- or 9-inch square baking pan. Place in a preheated 450-degree oven to melt. Meanwhile, combine cornmeal, baking powder, and salt in a medium bowl. Mix egg and milk; add to the dry ingredients. Mix until smooth. Spoon the batter into the preheated pan. Bake for 20 to 25 minutes, until the bread is golden brown and comes away from the sides of the pan. Cool in the pan on a wire rack. To serve, cut into squares. Serves 12.

Woodrow Wilson's Skillet Cornbread

Woodrow Wilson, 28th president of the United States, who led the nation through World War I and was an advocate of peace through the League of Nations, was of Scottish and Ulster-Scottish ancestry. The Woodrow Wilson Birthplace & Museum in Staunton, Virginia, is one of the few original presidential birthplaces open to the public. The Woodrow Wilson House, 2340 S Street NW, Washington, D.C., where the president moved after leaving the White House, is the only presidential museum in the nation's capital. It provides a glimpse into the life of an educator, scholar, and world statesman.

One of the president's favorite foods was a Virginia skillet cornbread, also called spider cornbread, as it was cooked in a heavy black frying pan with three short legs that sat on the hearth.

This version can be cooked in a skillet or baking dish.

2⅔ cups yellow or white cornmeal
⅔ cup all-purpose flour
2 tsp. baking powder
1 tsp. salt
3 to 4 tbsp. sugar
2 eggs, beaten
3 cups milk
¼ cup unsalted butter

Put cornmeal in a large bowl. Sift in flour, baking powder, salt, and sugar. Mix well. Combine eggs and 2 cups milk. Add to the dry ingredients. Melt butter in a medium skillet or round baking dish. Pour in the batter, tilting the skillet or dish to spread evenly. Pour remaining milk over the top. Do not stir. In a preheated 375-degree oven, bake at once for about 25 minutes, until cooked. To serve, cut into wedges. Top each with a pat of butter, if desired. Serves about 12.

Williamsburg Spoon Bread

In Williamsburg, Virginia, the 18th-century Christiana Campbell's Tavern, one of George Washington's favorite eating places, offers good food and historic surroundings. One of the traditional dishes is spoon bread, or batter bread, a soft, custardy dish usually made with cornmeal and served from the dish in which it is baked. The name is said to come from the custom of eating it with a spoon. It has long been a favorite food of Scottish Americans living in Virginia.

3 cups milk
1 cup water-ground cornmeal
2 tbsp. unsalted butter
3 eggs, beaten
1½ tsp. salt
3 tsp. baking powder

In a medium saucepan, combine 2 cups milk, the cornmeal, and butter over medium-high heat. Bring the mixture just to a boil, stirring constantly. Blend together eggs, salt, and remaining milk. Add to the cornmeal mixture; mix well. Stir in baking powder. Turn into a greased 1½-qt. baking dish. In a preheated 450-degree oven, bake for 35 minutes, until it tests done and is golden and puffed. Serve hot with butter. Serves 6 to 8.

Cakes and Cookies

"Nashville Is A Dining Town," proclaims the headline of the introduction to "Ward Belmont Specials," a booklet published in 1934 that contains a fascinating collection of recipes, including cakes, cookies, and icings. Founded on Christmas Day 1779, after Scotsman James Robertson and his followers established a settlement on the city's present site, Nashville, Tennessee has long been known for its prominent Scottish-American citizens and its focus on the preparation and enjoyment of superb food, including baked specialties.

James Robertson, best known as "The Father of Tennessee," planned and staged the city's first culinary event to celebrate the later arrival of boats bringing the wives, children, and older members of the group. Although their rations were depleted and the men had to turn to foraging in the unsettled wilderness, "the feast that Robertson and his men gave the half-starved newcomers about one'clock was one of the nation's great celebrations," wrote Alfred Leland Crabb in the booklet's introduction. "So began Nashville's commitment to the fine art of dining. And since that day, the settlement, the town, the city have had their attention focused on food, its production, its cooking and its serving."

Robertson was one of a great many Scots and Scotch-Irish pioneers who came from Virginia and the Carolinas through the mountains and valleys to Tennessee, bringing homeland traditions and recipes with them. While Nashville became known for its fine dining, the rugged homesteaders who built cabins in the mountain areas clung to simple pleasures of the past such as quilting and husking parties, fiddling, singing, and the enjoyment of homemade fare, including cakes and cookies, made with local foods.

With a rousing motto of "Grab Your Kilt and Head for the Hills!" Gatlinburg in east Tennessee celebrates its annual May Scottish Festival and Games with a weekend of activities. It begins with a mountain stroll on an easy trail in the Great Smoky Mountains, and there's always great food, including sausage rolls, *bridies*, and baked goods. More than 60 clan and heritage societies participate. The Scottish Celebration in The

Heart of Tennessee is held on the Middle Tennessee State University campus in Murfreesboro.

Many Scottish Americans have long been fond of the Moon Pie, two round cookies with marshmallow in between, which was created in 1917 by Sam H. Campbell, owner of the Chattanooga Bakery. A treasured Southern tradition that is eaten as a favorite snack with a soft drink, it is now made in a rainbow of chocolate-dipped colors and still sold at the bakery. Many Southerners regard the pie as a "cultural artifact."

Scottish cakes, originally made from doughs sweetened with honey and enhanced with dried fruits and spices, were like breads, and the words became confused because of the similarity of the ingredients. Even biscuits were called "biskcakes." For Scots in America, few pleasures were greater than homemade cakes, and the variety that came out of their kitchens is fascinating and amazing. Cookbooks devoted pages to cakes with all kinds of amusing and inspirational names, including those of notable persons. Imitations of the white cake Mary Todd prepared for her husband, Abraham Lincoln, became standard fare in Kentucky homes. Especially popular in the 19th century was the Gen. Robert E. Lee Cake, a sponge layer cake with a citrus-fruit-flavored filling and icing. The Scottish-American Confederate commander was said to have been very fond of the cake, and adaptations of it are still published.

Cake recipes in *The Shaw House Cook Book*, published by the Missouri Botanical Garden, are typical of those served during the mid-1800s in the town and country mansions of Henry Shaw, a St. Louis cutlery magnate, real-estate operator, and philanthropist. One of Shaw's favorites was Orange Ring Cake, made in a tube pan and topped with a warm orange syrup.

In every Scottish-American home, it was a pleasure to make cookies, especially with whole-grain oats and sometimes ginger. And the penchant for giving cookies whimsical names such as Hermits, Kisses, Snickerdoodles, and Rocks came from homemakers gathering and cooking in family kitchens and having fun. Exciting new cookie recipes are still being created.

Scottish Americans enjoy their characteristic shortbreads, cakes, and cookies as snacks, with afternoon tea, for special and family celebrations, and often as symbols of hospitality or "welcomes" for neighbors and friends.

Here is an inviting collection of recipes for many of the favorites.

Shortbread

Shortbread, sometimes called Scotch cake, is a unique Scottish creation. While not a bread or a cake, it isn't quite a cookie either. Perhaps it is best described as a rich, slightly sweet cookie-type cake with a pleasing flavor and a texture that is crisp and somewhat crumbly.

Possibly originating as a large, flat round of dough made with oatmeal and water and baked on a griddle, shortbread has been known in Scotland for centuries. Scottish immigrants introduced shortbread to America, and there are many early recipes for it. One states that "to be good," it "must be very brittle." Southerners used brown instead of the traditional white sugar. In Kentucky, the shortbread came to be known as Derby Cake, cut in wedges or squares and dusted with confectioners' sugar or topped with strawberries and cream. A variety called short'nin' or shortnin' bread was probably not shortbread but a quick bread made with shortening such as butter or lard.

Although there are now many kinds of shortbread, the traditional rich and "short" one is made with only flour, sugar, and plenty of butter (no substitutes). Its preparation requires skill and patience, for the ingredients must be blended perfectly, shaped carefully, and cooked exactly. Purists insist that the ingredients be worked together by hand or with the fingertips until they cling together and can be shaped into a ball. The dough should be baked slowly and quite long to have a sandy hue or pale golden color but not be brown.

While shortbread is made in various forms, from bars and wedges to rings and squares, the typical one is finger shaped. Some rounds of dough are baked in circular wooden or glazed earthenware molds stamped with a thistle, heather, flower, or other Scottish symbol, which leaves a raised pattern on the cooked shortbread.

Regardless of the shape, all shortbreads are pricked over the top with a fork before being baked. This prevents the dough from blistering. Some are also notched or pinched around the edges.

A plate of shortbread is a symbol of hospitality. Although enjoyed throughout the year in Scottish-American homes, shortbread is associated particularly with the Yule season, Christmas and Hogmanay, as well as other holidays. It goes well with just about everything, from tea to whisky, and ice cream to fruit.

Although shortbread in tartan-patterned or other color-fully designed tins or boxes is widely available, nothing compares to the marvelous aroma and flavor of home-baked shortbread made with a family or favorite recipe.

Petticoat Tails

This flat round of shortbread has a central circle and the rest divided into wedges to represent the skirt panels of women's petticoats of the 19th century, hence the name.

½ **cup (1 stick) unsalted butter, softened**
¼ **cup granulated sugar**
1 cup all-purpose flour
½ **cup cornstarch**
⅛ **tsp. salt**
Confectioners' sugar

In a large bowl, cream butter and sugar until light and fluffy. Gradually sift in flour, cornstarch, and salt, mixing. Combine thoroughly, preferably with the fingers or a wooden spoon, until the mixture is uniformly crumbly and can be pressed together to form a ball.

Place in the center of a lightly floured ungreased baking sheet. Roll or pat into a circle to a ¹/₈-inch thickness. With a floured cookie cutter or glass, cut out a 3-inch round in the center. Do not remove. With a floured sharp knife, cut the outer circle into 8 wedges to form "petticoat tails." Prick all over the top with a fork. In a preheated 300-degree oven, bake for about 20 minutes, until sandy white and firm to the touch. With a spatula, remove at once to a wire rack. Sprinkle with confectioners' sugar. To serve, arrange wedges around the center round on a serving plate. Makes 8 wedges and 1 round.

Church Social Strawberry Shortcake

A short biscuit dough, made with butter or shortening and then covered with fresh berries and cream, was made in several variations by Scottish-American cooks. One recipe suggested serving it "cut into triangles like pie, and sweet cream poured over each slice." Another directed that it "be sent to the table whole . . . or cut into square slices, and piled upon a plate." Each was a star attraction at glorious summer socials, standard church fundraising events, and community gatherings. Here is a traditional recipe.

1 qt. fresh strawberries
¾ cup plus 2 tbsp. granulated sugar
2 cups sifted all-purpose flour
1 tbsp. baking powder
1 tsp. salt
½ cup (1 stick) unsalted butter or shortening
¾ cup milk
About 2 tbsp. unsalted butter, softened
1 cup heavy cream, whipped
¼ cup confectioners' sugar

Wash and hull strawberries, reserving 6 for a garnish. Slice berries into a bowl. Cover with ³/₄ cup sugar. Mix well. Set aside. Sift flour, baking powder, 2 tbsp. sugar, and the salt into a large bowl. With a pastry blender, cut in butter or shortening until the mixture is uniformly crumbly. Pour in milk. Mix quickly with a fork. Turn out onto a floured board. Knead briefly. Divide the dough into 2 halves. Pat or roll each gently into a round large enough to fit into a greased 8-inch cake pan. Spread top of each with softened butter. Put 1 section of the dough on top of the other in the pan. In a preheated 450-degree oven, bake for 15 minutes, until golden brown and a tester inserted into the center comes out clean. Turn out onto a wire rack. Carefully cut crosswise into 2 halves. Put the bottom half on a large plate. Cover with half the sliced strawberries. Top with the second half of the cake and remaining sliced strawberries. Cover with whipped cream. Garnish with whole strawberries and sprinkle with confectioners' sugar. Serves 6 to 8.

Dundee Cake

Scotland's most famous light fruitcake, topped with its trademark almonds, is originally from Dundee, an old seaport northeast of Edinburgh. A favorite tea-time treat since the 1800s, it is treasured in America, where Scots enjoy the butter-rich cake for all special occasions, including those held in Dundee, Michigan.

1 cup (2 sticks) unsalted butter, softened
1 cup granulated sugar
5 eggs
2½ cups all-purpose flour
1 tsp. baking powder
½ tsp. salt
¾ cup dried black currants
¾ cup golden raisins
½ cup diced mixed candied fruit
½ cup ground blanched almonds
1 tbsp. grated orange zest
28 whole blanched almonds

In a large bowl, cream butter and sugar until light and fluffy. Add eggs, 1 at a time, beating after each addition. Sift in flour and baking powder and salt, adding alternately with currants, raisins, candied fruit, ground almonds, and orange zest. Mix thoroughly. Turn into a greased and lightly floured 8-inch round cake pan. Arrange whole almonds in concentric circles on top of the cake. In a preheated 300-degree oven, bake for 1½ hours, until a tester inserted into the center comes out clean. Let cool in the pan for 10 minutes. Remove from pan. Put on a wire rack to cool. Wrap in foil. Leave in a cool dry place to "mellow" for a few days. Or store in an airtight container. To serve, cut into slices. Makes 1 8-inch round cake.

Scone Cake

This is an excellent cake made with a sconelike dough and filled with jam to serve for an afternoon tea.

2 cups all-purpose flour
2 tbsp. granulated sugar
1 tbsp. baking powder
¾ tsp. salt
½ cup (1 stick) unsalted butter, diced
1 egg, beaten
About ⅓ cup milk

Filling and Topping

¾ cup raspberry or strawberry jam
2 tbsp. unsalted butter, softened
2 tbsp. granulated sugar

In a large bowl, thoroughly combine flour, sugar, baking powder, and salt. With a pastry blender, cut in butter until the mixture is uniformly crumbly. Make a well in the center of the dry ingredients. Add egg and enough milk to make a soft and sticky dough. Gather into a ball. Place on a lightly floured surface. With floured hands, knead gently. Divide the dough into 2 parts. Roll 1 into a 10-inch circle. Transfer to a lightly greased baking sheet. Spread the top evenly with jam. Roll the second part into a 10-inch circle. Carefully place over the jam-covered circle. Spread the top evenly with softened butter. Sprinkle lightly with sugar. In a preheated 400-degree oven, bake for about 18 minutes, until golden and puffed. Remove to a wire rack. Allow to cool slightly, about 5 minutes. To serve, cut with a sharp knife into 8 wedges. Serve warm. Serves 8.

Franklin Apple Cake

All Americans of Scottish descent will enjoy a visit to the mountains of Franklin, North Carolina, where the town has a number of annual programs and events, including a Taste of Scotland, to demonstrate the role of the Scots in traditional southern Appalachian culture. Here also, on Main Street, is the Scottish Tartans Museum and Heritage Center. The only museum of its kind in the United States, its purpose is to educate the public about the tartan and to carry on the work of the Scottish Tartans Society.

One of the local dishes I enjoyed while in Franklin was a tasty apple cake.

2 cups all-purpose flour
1½ tsp. baking powder
½ tsp. salt
½ cup (1 stick) unsalted butter, diced
4 medium tart, firm cooking apples, peeled,
  cored, and chopped
½ cup granulated sugar
⅛ tsp. freshly grated or ground nutmeg
1 egg
⅓ to ½ cup milk

Sift flour, baking powder, and salt into a large bowl. With a pastry blender, cut in butter until the mixture is uniformly crumbly.

In a medium bowl, combine apples, sugar, and nutmeg. Add to flour-butter mixture. In a small bowl, whisk egg and ⅓ cup milk. Add to apple mixture. Mix well. If needed, add more milk to make a fairly thick batter. Spoon into a greased 8- or 9-inch square baking pan. In a preheated 350-degree oven, bake for about 50 minutes, until a tester inserted into the center comes out clean. Cool in the pan on a wire rack. Cut into squares. Serve warm with cream or cold with whipped cream or ice cream, if desired. Makes 9 squares.

Orange Marmalade Cake

One of Scotland's great culinary achievements and an outstanding contribution to the breakfast table is a bittersweet golden shred or chip marmalade sold in distinctive stoneware jars. It was the creation of Scotswoman Janet Keiller, the wife of a Dundee merchant, who decided to sweeten and cook some leftover imported oranges that the locals found too sour for their taste. Scottish Americans enjoy the marmalade as a spread for toast, oatcakes, and scones and in a favorite dessert cake.

5 tbsp. unsalted butter, softened
½ cup granulated sugar
2 eggs
1 cup all-purpose flour
1½ tsp. baking powder
¼ tsp. baking soda
½ tsp. ground cinnamon
¼ tsp. salt
½ cup buttermilk
1 tsp. grated orange zest
½ tsp. vanilla extract
1 cup orange marmalade

With a pastry brush, coat the bottom and sides of a 9 x 5 x 3-inch loaf pan with 1 tbsp. butter. In a large bowl, cream remaining butter and sugar until light and fluffy. Add eggs, 1 at a time, beating after each addition. Sift in flour, baking powder and soda, cinnamon, and salt, adding alternately with buttermilk and beating until well blended. Stir in orange zest and vanilla. Mix well.

In a small saucepan, heat marmalade. Pour into buttered loaf pan, spreading evenly. Add the batter, spreading evenly. In a preheated 350-degree oven, bake for about 45 minutes, until a tester inserted into the center comes out clean. Cool in the pan for 10 minutes. Run a sharp knife around the edges. Carefully invert to a serving plate. Serve warm or cool. Serves 6 to 8.

Oatmeal Gingerbread

The scent that many Scottish Americans associate with childhood eating is ginger, a reminder of making and baking an assortment of family treats flavored with the aromatic spice, especially cookies, cakes, and breads. Gingerbread is simply a cake or cookie made from a batter or dough with a distinctive ginger taste. Brown sugar or molasses, dark sweeteners both for their deep taste and color, adds a unique flavor.

Scots have dozens of recipes for gingerbread in various forms and with a wide range of ingredients. This recipe is for moist squares of oatmeal gingerbread.

1 cup dark molasses
½ cup granulated sugar
½ cup (1 stick) unsalted butter, cut in small
   pieces
1 egg
1 cup milk
2¼ cups all-purpose flour

2 tsp. baking powder
1 tsp. ground ginger
½ tsp. ground cinnamon
½ tsp. salt
2 cups rolled oats

In a small saucepan, combine molasses, sugar, and butter over medium-high heat, stirring occasionally, until butter melts. Remove from heat. In a small bowl, whisk egg. Add milk; whisk again. Gradually add to molasses mixture.

Sift flour, baking powder, ginger, cinnamon, and salt into a large bowl. Gradually add molasses-milk mixture. Mix until smooth. Stir in oats; mix well. Turn into a greased 9-inch square baking pan, spreading evenly. In a preheated 350-degree oven, bake for about 40 minutes, until a tester inserted into the center comes out clean. Cool in the pan on a wire rack for 10 minutes. Remove from pan. Cool completely on the rack. Wrap in foil. To serve, cut into squares. Makes 1 square cake.

Oatmeal Cake

There are many recipes for this old-time Scottish-American favorite in the cookbooks of our forefathers. It is a pleasantly chewy cake and has a good texture. Some of these cakes are baked plain, others with a butter-nut topping. This is one variation.

Cake

1¼ cups boiling water
1 cup rolled oats
½ cup (1 stick) unsalted butter
1 cup granulated sugar

1 cup light brown sugar, firmly packed
2 eggs
1½ cups all-purpose flour
1 tsp. baking soda
1 tsp. ground cinnamon
¼ tsp. ground nutmeg
½ tsp. salt
1 cup raisins

Topping

3 tbsp. unsalted butter, melted
⅓ cup warm honey
1 cup minced walnuts or pecans
½ cup grated unsweetened coconut

In a small bowl, pour boiling water over oats. Let stand for 20 minutes. In a large bowl, cream butter and sugar with a wooden spoon until thoroughly blended. Add eggs. Mix well. Sift in flour, baking soda, cinnamon, nutmeg, and salt. Mix well. Stir in oats. Add raisins. Mix ingredients. Do not beat. Turn into a lightly floured and buttered 9-inch square baking pan. In a preheated 350-degree oven, bake for 50 minutes, until a tester inserted into the center comes out clean. Remove from oven. Turn on the broiler.

Meanwhile, in a small bowl combine the topping ingredients. Spread on the hot cake. Place under the broiler for 2 to 3 minutes, until the topping is bubbly and golden. Watch carefully so it does not burn. Remove cake from oven. Cool in the pan for 10 minutes. Turn out of the pan onto a wire rack. Cool. Cut into squares. Serves 10 to 12.

Lemon Sponge Cake

This tea-time cake, flavored with cinnamon and lemon, is a traditional Scottish specialty.

½ cup (1 stick) unsalted butter, softened
1 cup granulated sugar
4 eggs
1 tsp. grated lemon zest
2 cups all-purpose flour
2 tsp. baking powder
½ tsp. ground cinnamon
¼ tsp. salt
Confectioners' sugar

In a large bowl, cream butter and sugar until light and fluffy. Add eggs, 1 at a time, beating after each addition. Stir in lemon zest. Sift in flour, baking powder, cinnamon, and salt. Beat until smooth. Pour the batter into a greased and floured 9 x 5 x 3-inch loaf pan. In a preheated 350-degree oven, bake for 1 hour, or until a tester inserted into the center comes out clean. Cool in the pan for 5 minutes. Turn out on a wire rack to cool. Dust the top with confectioners' sugar. To serve, cut into thin slices. Makes 1 loaf.

Melting Moments

These delicate little cakes are so tender that they practically melt in the mouth, thus the name. Serve for afternoon tea or with ice cream or a light pudding. In some Southern states they are called Kisses.

¾ cup (1½ sticks) unsalted butter, softened
½ cup granulated sugar
1 tsp. grated lemon zest
2 cups cornstarch
1 tsp. baking powder
2 eggs, beaten
Confectioners' sugar

In a large bowl, cream butter and sugar until light and fluffy. Mix in lemon zest. Sift in cornstarch and baking powder, adding a little at a time alternately with eggs, mixing well after each addition to make a light and creamy batter. Spoon by teaspoonfuls into buttered miniature-muffin pans. In a preheated 425-degree oven, bake for 12 to 15 minutes, until a tester inserted into the center comes out clean and the cakes are a delicate golden color. With a knife, cut around the edges. Carefully remove from the pan to wire racks. Cool. Serve sprinkled with confectioners' sugar. Makes 2½ dozen.

Oatmeal Cookies

Oatmeal cookies have long been one of America's favorite treats, and some Scots believe that they originated in Scotland as small, round, and flat oatcakes. In fact, the *Clan Douglas Cookbook* says that oatmeal cookies are the "world's oldest cookie recipe" and also claims that the word "cookie" originated in Scotland in the year 1730. One learns interesting things from Scottish-American clan cookbooks.

These crisp, rich cookies have a marvelous flavor and texture.

½ cup (1 stick) unsalted butter
1 cup light brown sugar
1 egg
1 tsp. baking soda
3 tbsp. cold water
2 cups rolled oats
⅛ tsp. salt
1 cup all-purpose flour

In a large bowl, cream butter and sugar until light and fluffy. Add egg; mix well. Dissolve baking soda in the water. Add to the creamed mixture. Stir in oats and salt, mixing thoroughly. Add flour, ¹/₂ cup at a time, enough to make a stiff dough. Separate into 2 parts. Wrap each in waxed paper. Refrigerate for 2 hours.

After chilling, roll out each part on a floured board to a thickness of about ¹/₄ inch. With a floured 2¹/₂-inch cutter, cut into rounds. Transfer rounds to ungreased baking sheets. In a preheated 400-degree oven, bake for 8 to 10 minutes, until set and firm to the touch. Transfer to wire racks. Cool. Serve or store in an airtight container. Makes about 2 dozen.

Note: For smaller cookies, cut into 2-inch rounds.

Grandfather Mountain Oaties

Grandfather Mountain in Linville, North Carolina, the highest and most spectacular peak in the Blue Ridge, is so named because its profile resembles a bearded old man looking toward the sky. It is well known as the site of the largest Scottish clan gathering in the Eastern United States. Established by a group of Scottish descendants and members of the MacRae family, the Highland Games & Gathering of the Scottish Clans has been held since 1956 on the second weekend in July at MacRae Meadows near the entrance to the mountain.

These oatmeal cookies from North Carolina are favorite snacks at the Games and at picnics on the mountain.

¼ **cup dark molasses**
½ **cup (1 stick) unsalted butter, diced**
¼ **cup granulated sugar**
1 **cup all-purpose flour**
1 **tsp. baking powder**
½ **tsp. baking soda**
½ **tsp. salt**
1 **cup plus 3 tbsp. rolled oats**

In a small saucepan, combine molasses, butter, and sugar over medium-high heat, stirring occasionally, until butter melts. Remove from heat. Sift flour, baking powder and soda, and salt into a large bowl. Stir in 1 cup oats. Add molasses-butter mixture. Mix well. Spoon into a greased 9-inch square baking pan, spreading evenly. Sprinkle the top with remaining oats. In a preheated 375-degree oven, bake for 20 minutes, until golden and firm. Cut into squares. Cool in the pan for 10 minutes. Remove to a wire rack. Cool. Makes 16 squares.

Mincemeat Oat Squares

The preparation of mincemeat, a blend of dried and fresh fruit, spices, brown sugar, cider, and sometimes meat, has been an important annual ritual in many Scottish-American homes. Early cookbooks reveal that it was made with a diverse selection of local foods, prepared in large quantities, and used to make pies as well as breads and cookies. While over the years many versions of homemade mincemeat were created, commercially prepared mincemeat is readily available in convenient forms and can be used in these cake-cookie squares.

1½ cups all-purpose flour
1 cup rolled oats
⅓ cup light brown sugar, firmly packed
¼ tsp. freshly grated or ground nutmeg
½ tsp. salt
¾ cup unsalted butter, cold and diced
2 cups ready-to-use or homemade mincemeat
1 cup chopped blanched almonds

In a large bowl, combine flour, oats, sugar, nutmeg, and salt. With a pastry blender, cut in butter until the mixture is crumbly. Spoon ¾ of the mixture into a buttered 8- or 9-inch square baking pan, spreading evenly. Top with mincemeat, spreading evenly. Combine almonds and the remaining mixture. Sprinkle evenly over the top. In a preheated 400-degree oven, bake for 25 to 30 minutes, until the top is golden and crisp. Cool. Cut into squares. Serve with ice cream, if desired. Makes 9 squares.

Desserts

Georgetown was a thriving community before the city of Washington, the nation's capital, of which it is now a part, was even a dream. It had lovely Georgian and Federal mansions, prosperous businesses, and taverns of such quality as to attract notable persons. In the first years of its existence, the historic town was owned and operated by resourceful Scots, who gave it a bonnie good beginning.

Although there is little evidence of it today, Georgetown has a remarkable Scots background. It was a place where Scottish Americans lived, worked, and entertained with fine fare, including delectable desserts.

A group of canny Scots as early as the 17th century recognized the assets of this 60-acre plot along the Potomac River. For here the river was deep enough for stately sailing ships to dock, the current washed down stones from the falls above to use for paving the streets, and the rich clay for making bricks abounded. Here also the Indians came downstream by canoe to trade their produce, and here the Virginia and Maryland planters came by boat and wagon with their crops.

Two of the original Scottish landowners were Ninian Beall and George Gordon. A Scot, Robert Peter, became the first mayor.

By 1791, the city of "George Town" was an important trading center, and handsome homes designed by notable architects in the Federal style were being carefully built with expansive grounds on the Heights, as Upper Georgetown was called by prosperous Scottish Americans. Today these buildings provide a remarkable record of the Scottish legacy. Particularly outstanding is Tudor Place, circa 1805, a handsome yellow stucco mansion surrounded by acres of formal gardens, located on the crest of a hill rising from Q Street at 31st Street. Exceptional for its beauty, it was owned by Martha Washington's granddaughter and namesake, Martha Parke Custis, and her husband, Thomas Peter, son of Robert and a well-to-do merchant and banker. The couple entertained with brilliant social events attended by dignitaries, including George Washington and John Adams. Now a national historic landmark, the home, occupied by succeeding generations of the Peter family until 1983, is the most significant surviving 19th-century residence in Washington.

In Georgetown homes, Scottish Americans have always entertained by serving marvelous desserts. As elsewhere across the country, they have a traditional passion for all things sweet. Their desserts are luscious, ranging from foamy light creams and silken-smooth custards to elaborate puddings and pastries.

Among the treasured array of cold sweets brought from Scotland to America are those made with cream, eggs, and flavorings, often including a generous lacing of spirits. In his novel *The Bride of Lammermoor,* Sir Walter Scott describes a dinner with desserts that were "a fairy feast of cream, jellies, strawberries, almond-cream, and lemon-cream."

Here are recipes for some desserts favored by Scottish Americans.

Caledonian Cream

This traditional dessert is flavored with two favorite Scottish treasures, orange marmalade and Drambuie.

½ cup orange marmalade
3 tbsp. Drambuie
2 tsp. fresh lemon juice
2 cups heavy cream, chilled
3 tbsp. confectioners' sugar

In a small bowl, combine marmalade, Drambuie, and lemon juice. Leave at room temperature for 30 minutes.

In a chilled large bowl, whip cream until soft peaks form. Gradually add sugar. Whip until the mixture thickens. Fold in marmalade mixture. Spoon into 6 stemmed glasses, dividing equally. Garnish tops with a bit of orange peel from marmalade, if desired. Refrigerate for up to 2 hours. Serves 6.

Raspberry Fool

Early Scottish Americans were fond of a light cream dessert called a fool, made simply with a puree of sweetened fruit, whipped cream, and usually a flavoring such as a liqueur. The origin of the name is not certain. At one time it was synonymous with the word trifle, meaning something of little consequence or, perhaps, a bit foolish. Scots trifle, a layered arrangement of ladyfingers or cake, custard, fruit jam, and whipped cream, was generally flavored with wine or liquor. An old Yule specialty served attractively in a handsome glass bowl, it is also called Tipsy Laird (Lord) by Scottish Americans, because of its alcoholic content. One early American recipe for a fool is made with tart, pale-green gooseberries, which have an agreeable acidic sweetness. Fools can be made with all kinds of berries, including the raspberries used to make this colorful dessert.

3 cups fresh raspberries
½ cup sugar, preferably superfine
3 tbsp. Drambuie
1½ cups heavy cream, chilled
Whole raspberries, for garnish

In a blender or food processor, puree raspberries with ¼ cup sugar. Turn into a large bowl. Stir in Drambuie. In a large chilled bowl, whip cream until large, soft peaks form. Gradually add remaining sugar. Whip until the mixture thickens. Fold in raspberry puree. Spoon into a glass bowl or 6 stemmed dessert glasses, dividing equally. Garnish the tops with 1 or 2 whole raspberries. Refrigerate for up to 2 hours. Serves 6.

Syllabub

A syllabub or sillyboo is, like a fool, a delectable cream dessert but usually includes wine or brandy. In early America, cider was often a favorite ingredient. No one seems to know where the silly name comes from, although it might have meant the same thing as fool. In the American South, the syllabub became very popular and was served as a drink as well as a dessert. The milk, or cream, was often drawn directly while warm and frothy from a cow into a serving bowl. One amusing early American recipe, "To make a fine Syllabub from the Cow," read: "Sweeten a quart of cyder with double refined sugar, grate nutmeg into it, then milk your cow into your liquor."

In the South, Scottish-Americans made a syllabub called Everlasting, prepared so it would not separate and would last longer, and another called "whipt" that included beaten sweetened egg whites and was served in special glasses. Mary Randolph's recipe for syllabub read simply: "Season the milk with sugar and white wine, but not enough to curdle it; fill the glasses nearly full, and crown them with whipt cream seasoned."

Syllabubs must be whipped until frothy, which can be done with a wire whisk or electric beater. There is also a cylindrical copper syllabub churn that is sold in some specialty shops.

Here is a recipe for my favorite syllabub.

Grated zest and juice of 1 large lemon
½ cup dry white wine
½ cup brandy
2 cups heavy cream, chilled
¼ cup sugar, preferably superfine
Freshly grated nutmeg, to taste

In a small bowl, combine lemon zest and juice, wine, and brandy. Leave at room temperature for about 1 hour. Strain.

In a chilled large bowl, whip cream until soft peaks form.

Gradually add sugar and wine mixture. Whip until the mixture thickens. Spoon into 6 stemmed dessert glasses, dividing equally. Garnish the tops with a little nutmeg. Serve at once or refrigerate for up to 2 hours. Serves 6.

Cranachan

Scotland's national pudding, called cranachan or crowdie cream, is a traditional folk dessert once prepared for harvest celebrations and holidays, made with a mixture of oatmeal, sweetened whipped cream, whatever berries were in season, and whisky. Scottish Americans hail it as a favorite Highland dish that they prepare with family recipes for special occasions.

This is one version that is made preferably with nutritious fresh blueberries.

½ cup rolled oats
1 cup heavy cream, chilled
2 tbsp. sugar
2 tbsp. Scotch whisky
2 cups fresh blueberries or other berries

Spread oats in a shallow baking pan. In a preheated 350-degree oven, toast oats, stirring occasionally, for about 15 minutes, until light golden brown. Remove from oven. Cool.

In a chilled large bowl, whip cream until soft peaks form. Gradually add sugar and whisky. Whip until the mixture thickens. Fold in oats.

Layer the cream mixture and berries in 4 dessert glasses, beginning with a layer of cream and topping with a layer of berries. Refrigerate for up to 2 hours. Serves 4.

Atholl Brose

On a balmy summer evening while dining at my home, I was discussing traditional Scotch desserts with my guest and friend, Anne Robertson Kennedy, president of the Living Legacy of Scotland in Washington, D.C., affiliated with the Scottish Coalition.

Anne recalled a great dessert, Atholl Brose, served traditionally as a drink but also as a honey- and whisky-flavored cream.

Here is a recipe for one of the many versions.

1 pt. heavy cream
⅓ cup Scotch whisky
2 to 3 tbsp. honey, preferably heather
⅓ cup toasted oats

In a large bowl, whip cream until thick. Gradually add whisky, whipping until cream holds its shape. Add honey to taste. Stir in oats. Chill. Serve in stemmed glasses. Serves 4.

Strawberry Flummery

A dessert that originated in Scotland as an oatmeal pottage called frumenty became over the years a sweet pudding made in many variations, including one with berries. Some Scottish Americans call it a berry pudding or flummery.

½ cup plus 2 tbsp. sugar
⅓ cup cornstarch
¼ tsp. salt
4 cups milk
2 egg yolks, beaten
2 tsp. vanilla extract
1 pt. fresh strawberries, washed, hulled, and
   sliced lengthwise

In a medium saucepan, combine ½ cup sugar, the cornstarch, and salt. Gradually add milk, stirring. Cook over medium-high heat, stirring, until the mixture bubbles and thickens. In a small dish, combine 3 or 4 tbsp. of the hot mixture with egg yolks. Stir into the hot mixture. Cook slowly, stirring, for about 2 minutes, until thickened and smooth. Remove from heat and cool. Add vanilla. Turn into a serving bowl. Cover with plastic wrap. Refrigerate for 2 to 3 hours, until set. Just before serving, sprinkle sliced strawberries with remaining sugar. Carefully arrange over the top of the chilled custard. Serves 8.

Blanc Mange with Strawberries

A cold milk pudding meaning "white food," thickened with cornstarch and covered with fruit or a sweet sauce, was one of Thomas Jefferson's favorite desserts that he served at Monticello. Sometimes called cold shape, it was a popular Southern Scottish-American specialty served as an elegant "company dessert."

3 cups milk
½ cup sugar
5 tbsp. cornstarch
¼ tsp. salt
1 tsp. vanilla extract
1½ cups sweetened, sliced fresh strawberries

In the top of a double boiler over simmering hot water, scald 2½ cups milk. In a small bowl, combine remaining milk with sugar, cornstarch, and salt. Pour in a little of the hot milk; mix well. Add to the scalded milk. Cook slowly, stirring occasionally, for about 15 minutes, until thickened and smooth. Remove from heat. Cool slightly. Stir in vanilla. Turn into a large bowl. Refrigerate to chill. Serve in individual dessert dishes topped with strawberries. Serves 4.

Floating Islands

An early Scottish-American dessert was a light custard pudding that was served topped with meringue "floats," thus the name.

4 eggs
10 tbsp. sugar
1½ tsp. vanilla extract
3 cups milk, scalded
Salt, to taste

Separate 2 of the eggs. Set aside the whites to be used as "floats." In the top of a double boiler over simmering hot water, combine 2 egg yolks, 2 whole eggs, 4 tbsp. sugar, and ¼ tsp. vanilla. Gradually add milk. Cook over medium-low heat, stirring almost constantly, until the custard coats a metal spoon. Remove from heat. Stir in 1 tsp. vanilla. Turn into a large bowl. Cool and then chill in the refrigerator.

While the custard is cooling, beat the 2 egg whites in a chilled large bowl until foamy. Gradually add remaining sugar and a pinch of salt. Beat until stiff. Add remaining vanilla. In a shallow baking dish, pour in boiling water to a depth of 1 inch. Drop the beaten egg-white mixture by tablespoons on top of the water. In a preheated 325-degree oven, bake for 10 minutes. With a slotted spoon, remove to a plate. Serve the chilled custard topped with the meringue "floats." Serves 4 to 6.

Sarasota Sweet-Potato Pudding

The charming city and cultural center of Sarasota, Florida, has a proud Scottish heritage dating back to the late 1880s when Scots laid out the plans for the town. Many Scottish Americans became prominent civic leaders and businessmen there. Now a popular sport, golf was introduced from Scotland to Florida, and the first course was laid out in Sarasota in 1886.

Among the city's culinary attractions at Scottish clan meetings and gatherings are traditional desserts and sometimes a spicy sweet pudding that Scots make with the nutritious Southern favorite, the sweet potato.

2 cups mashed cooked or canned sweet potatoes
⅓ cup honey
2 eggs, separated
¼ cup milk
½ tsp. ground cinnamon
¼ tsp. ground allspice
½ tsp. salt
2 tbsp. melted unsalted butter
2 tbsp. brandy (optional)
½ cup chopped pecans

In a large bowl, combine sweet potatoes and honey. In a small bowl, combine egg yolks and milk. Mix well. Stir in cinnamon, allspice, salt, butter, brandy, and pecans, mixing well. Add to sweet potatoes. In another large bowl, whip egg whites until stiff. Fold into the sweet-potato mixture. Spoon into a buttered 1½-qt. baking dish. In a preheated 350-degree oven, bake until set, about 50 minutes. Serve warm with cream, if desired. Serves 6.

Ice Cream

"I scream, you scream, we all scream for ice cream." Yes, we all love it and enjoy ice cream in fascinating desserts made with marvelous flavors.

Nobody knows exactly when ice cream was first introduced to America from Europe. By the mid-1700s, however, the frozen specialty was enjoyed only by wealthy and prominent persons. A Scottish American named William Black, after dining at the Annapolis home of Maryland's governor, Thomas Bladen, made the first known reference to the delicacy and is credited with coining the phrase ice cream. In his journal, Black wrote that he had dined on a "Dessert no less Curious; among the Rarities of which it was Compos'd was some fine Ice Cream which, with the Strawberries and Milk, eat most deliciously."

George Washington was fond of ice cream, and Thomas Jefferson astonished guests by serving it in a pastry shell. Dolley Madison, whose mother was first cousin to Patrick Henry, was the wife of James Madison, our fourth president and a prominent Scottish American. She became our nation's first political hostess and is credited with popularizing ice cream after serving it at most of her White House receptions. At one of them, she created a sensation with strawberry ice cream. In the center of the beautifully set table was "high on a silver platter, a large shining dome of pink Ice Cream."

Mary Randolph gave us our first printed recipes for several kinds of ice cream, ranging from almond and coconut to quince and vanilla.

Following is a recipe for a colorful ice-cream dessert.

Strawberry-Vanilla Ice Cream Pie

This easy-to-prepare pie can be kept in the freezer, ready to serve for an impromptu dessert.

1 baked 9-inch pastry shell
1 qt. vanilla ice cream, softened
1 cup chopped walnuts
1 10-oz. pkg. frozen strawberries, partially
  thawed
Whipped cream

Chill pastry shell. In a bowl, combine ice cream and walnuts. Spoon half the mixture into the pie shell, spreading evenly. Spread the top with ³/₄ of the strawberries. Cover with remaining ice cream and walnuts. Chill in the freezer for a few minutes. Top with remaining strawberries and garnish with whipped cream. Chill in the freezer until firm. When ready to serve, take out of the freezer and leave at room temperature for several minutes. Serves 6.

Apple Pie

No fruit was more important to early Scottish settlers than the apple. Raw or cooked, apples provided nutrition and variety to a limited diet, and apple pie, said to have been introduced by Scots, became America's favorite dessert. In pioneer days, pies made with dried apples nurtured generations of Scottish Americans. For those moving westward, pie houses offering "open-face, crossbar, and covered top" dried apple pies were treasured landmarks. Over the years, cooks created hundreds of apple pie recipes with fresh apples, and "as American as apple pie" became a popular phrase.

John McIntosh was the youngest son of a Scottish family that immigrated to America about 1776 and settled in upper New York. After a family dispute, he moved to Ontario, Canada, and in 1796 became a farmer along the St. Lawrence River. The McIntosh apple originated on his farm, near what is now Dundela. According to a plaque there, the original tree was "one of a number of seedlings . . . transplanted by John McIntosh in the year 1796." Soon, relatives in Vermont and New York planted the variety and sang its praises. Within a short time the McIntosh became the predominant apple of the Northeast.

John Chapman, better known as an eccentric folk hero called Johnny Appleseed, established a legend by traveling the sparsely settled trans-Appalachian frontier for nearly 50 years and planting apple seeds, preaching, praying, and doing good. Apples were scarce in those days and he was "intent only on making the wilderness fruitful."

Following is a recipe for apple pie.

Apple Crumb Pie

This pie is great for a holiday meal.

6 large tart apples, peeled and cored
1 unbaked 9-inch pastry shell
3 tbsp. granulated sugar
1 tsp. ground cinnamon
¼ tsp. ground nutmeg
⅛ tsp. salt
½ cup brown sugar
½ cup all-purpose flour
¼ cup (½ stick) unsalted butter

Cut apples into thin slices; arrange in pastry shell. In a small dish, combine granulated sugar, cinnamon, nutmeg, and salt. Sprinkle over apples. In a medium bowl, combine brown sugar and flour. With a pastry blender, cut in butter until the mixture is like fine crumbs. Sprinkle over apple mixture. In a preheated 400-degree oven, bake for 40 minutes, until apples are well done. Serve warm. Serves 6.

Apple Crisp

This dessert, also called a crumble, made with apples and a crunchy walnut-oat topping, has long been a favorite for Scottish-American informal meals. The secret to making it is flavorful, ripe Granny Smith apples.

5 large Granny Smith apples, peeled, cored, and sliced
1 tbsp. fresh lemon juice
1½ cups rolled oats
½ cup brown sugar, firmly packed
½ cup chopped walnuts
½ tsp. ground cinnamon
½ cup (1 stick) unsalted butter, cold and diced

In a medium bowl, toss apple slices and lemon juice. Arrange in a buttered 8- or 9-inch square baking dish. In a separate bowl, combine oats, brown sugar, walnuts, and cinnamon. With a pastry blender, cut in butter until the mixture is uniformly crumbly. Spread evenly over apples to make a topping. In a preheated 350-degree oven, bake for about 45 minutes, until apples are tender and top is golden and crisp. Serve warm with cream or vanilla ice cream, if desired. Serves 6.

Ozark Apple Pudding

Early Scottish settlers in the Ozark Mountain regions of Missouri planted apples of several varieties, and for years the area has been famous for apple desserts, including this pudding.

2 eggs, slightly beaten
1 cup brown sugar
½ cup all-purpose flour
2 tsp. baking powder
½ tsp. salt
1 tsp. vanilla extract
1 cup chopped walnuts
1 cup peeled, diced tart apples

In a large bowl, beat eggs and sugar until creamy. Sift in flour, baking powder, and salt. Add vanilla. Mix well. Stir in walnuts and apples. Spoon into a greased 10-inch pie plate. In a preheated 350-degree oven, bake for 30 minutes, until firm. Serve warm or cold with vanilla ice cream, if desired. Serves 6.

Stone Mountain Peach Shortcake

Stone Mountain, Georgia, a massive dome rising 825 feet above a surrounding 3,200-acre recreational and historic park, is located a short drive northeast of Atlanta. Among its many attractions are three colossal equestrian figures, Jefferson Davis, Gen. Thomas ("Stonewall") Jackson, and Gen. Robert E. Lee, all prominent Scottish Americans, sculpted on the mountain's sheer face and illuminated at night.

In October 2005, the 33rd annual Highland Games and Scottish Festival were held in the meadow of Stone Mountain Park. Scots from around the world came to celebrate at one of the country's liveliest Gatherings.

Scottish Americans use the peach, for which Georgia is famous, to make a number of desserts, including this shortcake and a cobbler that I first enjoyed while visiting Atlanta.

2 cups all-purpose flour
1 tbsp. baking powder
About 1¼ cups sugar
¼ tsp. salt
½ cup (1 stick) unsalted butter
¾ cup milk
3 tbsp. unsalted butter, softened
1 qt. peeled peach slices
1 cup heavy cream

Sift flour, baking powder, 3 tbsp. sugar, and salt into a large bowl. With a pastry blender, cut in butter until the mixture is uniformly crumbly. Add milk. Mix quickly just to combine the ingredients. Divide the dough into 2 halves. Pat or roll each half into a soft round to fit into a greased 8-inch layer-cake pan. Spread 1 layer with the softened butter. Top with another layer. In a preheated 450-degree oven, bake for about 15 minutes, until a tester inserted into the center comes out clean. Cool on a wire rack. Carefully split crosswise into halves.

In a bowl, combine peach slices and ³⁄₄ cup sugar. Spoon

most of the fruit between the layers. Top with remaining fruit. In a chilled large bowl, beat cream until stiff. Sweeten with sugar, about ¼ cup. Spoon over peaches. Serve at once. Serves 6 to 8.

Peach Cobbler

A deep-dish baked dessert made with sweetened fruit or berries and usually a biscuit topping is of Scottish origin. Some people say the name comes from the expression "to cobble up" or "to put together quickly." Others maintain it was because a cobbler's wife baked the original dish. Or perhaps because the top crust is thick and uneven, it resembles a cobblestone pavement. Scottish Americans make cobblers with a variety of fruits, particularly peaches and berries.

½ cup unsalted butter
½ cup granulated sugar
2 eggs
½ tsp. grated lemon zest
1 cup all-purpose flour
2 tsp. baking powder
¼ tsp. salt
2 cups peeled ripe peach slices
⅓ cup brown sugar
½ tsp. ground cinnamon

In a large bowl, cream butter and granulated sugar until light and fluffy. Add eggs and lemon zest. Mix well. Sift in flour, baking powder, and salt. Mix well. In another bowl, combine peaches, brown sugar, and cinnamon. Spread evenly in a shallow 8- or 9-inch square baking dish. Top with the batter, spreading evenly. In a preheated 375-degree oven, bake for about 30 minutes, until golden and crisp. Serve warm with the peach mixture spooned over the biscuit topping. Cover with cream, if desired. Serves 6.

Blueberry Cobbler

Here's the recipe for another Scottish-American cobbler.

¾ cup granulated sugar
1 egg
3 tbsp. melted unsalted butter
1 cup all-purpose flour
2 tsp. baking powder
½ tsp. salt
¼ cup milk
2 cups fresh blueberries
⅛ tsp. ground cinnamon

In a large bowl, combine ½ cup sugar and the egg. Mix well. Stir in butter. Sift in flour, baking powder, and salt, adding alternately with milk. Mix well. In a bowl, combine blueberries with the remaining sugar and cinnamon. Spread evenly in a greased 12 x 8 x 2-inch baking dish. Top with the batter, spreading evenly. In a preheated 375-degree oven, bake for 30 minutes, until a tester inserted into the center comes out clean. Serve warm, berry side up. Top with cream, a custard sauce, or vanilla ice cream, if desired. Serves 6.

Caramel Pears

The fine-grained and juicy pear, grown in many varieties, is a favorite Scottish-American fruit for making desserts. This is one of them.

3 firm large pears
6 tbsp. unsalted butter
6 tbsp. sugar
½ tsp. ground ginger
1 cup heavy cream
½ cup plain or toasted sliced almonds

Peel and halve pears lengthwise. Scoop out pit cores and cut out stems. Arrange pear halves in a shallow baking dish, cut side up. Put 1 tbsp. butter and 1 tbsp. sugar in the center of each pear half. Sprinkle with ginger. In a preheated 350-degree oven, bake, covered, for about 25 minutes, until tender. Remove pears to a serving dish. Cook the sugar-butter sauce that remains in the dish over medium-low heat until it turns golden brown. Stir in cream. Cook, stirring, for about 1 minute. Pour over pears. Sprinkle with almonds. Serve at once. Serves 6.

Butterscotch Pie

A popular flavoring made by combining butter, brown sugar, and usually lemon juice is called butterscotch because it is said to have originated in Scotland. Recipes for it are found in early Scottish cookbooks. Americans enjoy sauces, cakes, cookies, puddings, and pies flavored with it. Butterscotch is also a hard brittle candy.

¾ cup brown sugar
½ cup granulated sugar
⅓ cup all-purpose flour
2 cups milk, scalded
⅛ tsp. salt
3 eggs, separated
1½ tbsp. unsalted butter
1½ tsp. vanilla extract
1 baked 9-inch pastry shell

In the top of a double boiler over simmering hot water, combine brown sugar, ¼ cup granulated sugar, and flour. Gradually add milk, stirring to make a smooth mixture. Add salt. Cook, stirring occasionally, for 15 minutes, until thickened. In a small dish, spoon some of the hot mixture over egg yolks; mix well. Return to the double boiler. Cook for about 2 minutes, until thickened. Remove from heat; stir in butter; cool. Add 1 tsp. vanilla. Mix well. Spoon into pastry shell. In a large bowl, beat egg whites until stiff. Gradually beat in remaining granulated sugar and vanilla. Beat again. Spoon this meringue over the pie filling, spreading evenly to the edges.

In a preheated 350-degree oven, bake for about 12 minutes, until the meringue is golden. Cool. Serves 6 to 8.

Pecan Chess Pie

One of our oldest traditional pies, especially associated with the South and favored by Scottish Americans, is a rich custard type called chess pie, made with butter, eggs, a flavoring, and lots of sugar. It is also called sugar pie. One amusing tale about the name is that a waitress or cook, when asked about her favorite dessert, replied, "Jes' pie"—chess pie. Still another explanation is that the name came from the kitchen chest, or pie safe, in which pies and other baked goods were stored before the days of refrigeration.

In the South, the pies, first sweetened with molasses and then brown and white sugars, became popular for everyday and company meals. Several Southern states claimed the pie as a regional specialty and many variations of the recipe evolved. One of the best-known versions is called Jeff or Jefferson Davis Pie, named for the American statesman and president of the Confederacy, who was of Scottish ancestry on his mother's side. In addition to butter, brown sugar, egg yolks, cream, and flour, it includes raisins and nuts, perhaps dates, and spices and is sometimes topped with a meringue.

Here is a recipe for another favorite chess pie.

½ cup (1 stick) unsalted butter, softened
1 cup light brown sugar, firmly packed
½ cup granulated sugar
3 eggs
3 tbsp. light cream or milk
1 tsp. vanilla extract
1 cup chopped pecans
1 unbaked 9-inch pastry shell

In a medium bowl, cream butter and sugars until light and fluffy. Add eggs, 1 at a time, mixing well. Add cream or milk, vanilla, and pecans. Beat to mix well. Turn the mixture into pastry shell. In a preheated 375-degree oven, bake for 40 to 45 minutes, until the center is set but still soft. Cool on a wire rack before cutting. Serves 6 to 8.

Beverages

Early Scottish settlers in America enjoyed a great variety of captivating drinks that provided sustenance and pleasure. Some of them were introduced from Scotland and others created in their new homeland, where many of them remain esteemed libations.

Scottish Americans, like Scots around the world, have always liked to have a good time and enjoy the "social glass," as Robert Burns called the national drink, Scotch whisky. Drinking strong spirits is an important element of everyday living and all Scottish celebrations.

Certainly the best known of all the Scottish drinks is the world-famous Scotch whisky, a unique creation because it cannot be produced elsewhere. It derives its special character from Scotland's pure clear water, its superb barley and peat, and even its climate. The word whisky comes from the Gaelic *uisqebeatha* or *uisgebaugh*, for "water of life." The English shortened it to whisky (spelled without an *e*).

By the 15th century, the art of distilling malt was well established in the Scottish Highlands, where the drink was a fierce, smoky brew that came from pot stills.

Although Scotch is not produced in America, it has long been a favorite libation there. Today most Scotch whisky is a blend of the flavorful malt with a lighter cereal spirit, traditionally served as a cocktail, aperitif, and after-dinner drink. It is also a popular ingredient in mixed drinks. Pure whiskies from Scotland's individual distilleries are known as single (that is, unblended) malts. Long considered the aristocrats of Scotch, they are full-flavored, smooth, and assertive—like the Scots, some say. All single malts are best drunk neat, without ice, or, as they do in Scotland, with a splash of cool spring water to bring out the aroma. "These generous whiskies, with their individual flavors, recall the world of hills and glens, of raging elements, of shelter, of divine ease," wrote Neil Gunn.

It is not certain when American whisky was first made, but it is known that the most important contributions to the creation and development of the industry were made by Scotch-Irish and Scottish immigrants who arrived in America during the early 1700s to farm. Described as pioneers of "great energy, courage, and determination," they brought with them their stills and skills as distillers.

By the late 1700s, distilling had become an industry of prime importance in America. The farmers-distillers resisted payment of the federal excise tax, which resulted in the Whiskey Rebellion of 1794. They packed up and traveled to an area that George Washington called the "Country of Whiskey." The Scots took with them their homegrown traditions of whisky making, adapting them to grains, especially corn, that grew abundantly in the regions where they settled. They also discovered that whisky was a valuable commodity that could be traded for a variety of useful merchandise.

In 1789, the same year that George Washington took office as the first president of the United States, a frontier Scottish Baptist preacher named Elijah Craig began distilling a whisky made of corn mash instead of the traditional rye or barley used along the Eastern seaboard. At the time, he was running a paper and rope mill and a distillery on his farm at Royal Spring, a huge limestone spring near Lebanon, now Georgetown, Kentucky. The Craig family had come there from Virginia. According to local records, a fire swept through the building where the whisky barrels were being stored. Being something of a tightwad, the minister decided to fill the charred barrels with the corn and rye whisky he made. The color of the whisky changed, the flavor mellowed, and the reverend discovered the distinctive taste of a new drink. His customers liked it and named the drink for the Bourbon County in which it was made. Thus Elijah Craig is considered by many persons to be the "Father of Bourbon."

The Scott County Historical Society maintains a park at Royal Spring near Georgetown where there is a marker designating the "Birthplace of Bourbon" and a tribute to Craig as well as a statue of him. Elijah Craig Bourbon is produced at a distillery just south of Bardstown, Kentucky.

Craig's obituary stated, "If virtue consists of being useful to our fellow citizens, perhaps there are few more virtuous men than Mr. Craig."

Dr. James Crow, a physician who emigrated from Edinburgh, Scotland, to Kentucky in 1815, brought science to the production of bourbon by perfecting the sour-mash method of whisky making. Thus some people maintain that he is the inventor of bourbon. Old Crow Bourbon Whiskey is named for him.

America's most famous whisky is still made in Lynchburg, Tennessee, by relatives of the Scottish-Englishman Jack Daniel. Old Forrester Bourbon, the pride of Brown-Forman distillers, was founded by James Brown, of Scottish descent. Other early distilleries bore Scottish names such as Spears, Hamilton, and Stewart.

The Glenora Inn & Distillers complex is situated on a 200-acre site in the highlands of Inverness County, Cape Breton, Nova Scotia, only a few miles from the Atlantic, and is rich in Scottish culture. It is North America's only single-malt whisky distillery that uses the pot-distillation process. Conducted tours of the distillery are available to visitors. The inn's menu features Nova Scotia and Scottish specialties.

At the McCaskill Vineyard of Mendenhall, Mississippi, an unusual artisan muscadine wine is made by Gary T. McCaskill, who likes to give the drink to Scottish friends and neighbors.

Given below are recipes for and additional information about Scottish-American beverages.

Atholl Brose

This soothing whisky, oatmeal, and honey drink, sometimes enhanced with thick cream, is imbibed as a favorite
Scotch nightcap and sure cure for a cold. For many years it
has been the traditional drink "to warm the festive soul" at
Scottish-American celebrations, especially Hogmanay, Old
Year's Night. Most Scots have their favorite recipe for it,
sometimes kept secret.

In *Kidnapped*, Robert Louis Stevenson described the drink
as made of "old whisky, strained honey, and sweet cream
slowly beaten together in the right order and proportion!"
Most Scots use oats as an ingredient and consider cream an
optional choice.

There are many stories about the drink's origin. One is that
the Duke of Atholl, during the Highland rebellion in 1475,
poured the drink into the well of his archenemy, the Earl of
Ross, who "drunk deeply of it" and was thus easily captured.

Now there are many recipes for the drink. This one is said
to be the Duke of Atholl's recipe.

½ **cup rolled oats**
⅓ **cup water**
2 tbsp. heather honey
About 1 qt. Scotch whisky

In a small bowl, combine oats and water. Let stand for 1
hour. Strain into a bowl, pressing oats with a spoon. Discard
oats and transfer the liquid to a 1-qt. bottle. Add honey and
fill the bottle with whisky. Cover tightly and refrigerate or
keep cool. Shake well before serving. Makes 1 qt.

Auld Man's Milk

A morning beverage or pick-me-up made by combining cream, sugar, and egg yolks with whisky and beaten eggs was a Scottish creation called Auld Man's Milk. Introduced by Scottish Americans living in the South, it was served in a punch bowl or glasses, topped with grated nutmeg, and called eggnog.

6 eggs, separated
½ lb. sugar
1 qt. light cream
2 cups Scotch whisky
Freshly grated nutmeg

In a medium bowl, beat egg yolks until lemon-colored. Add sugar and cream, mixing well until sugar dissolves. Gradually add whisky. In a separate bowl, beat egg whites. Pour egg-yolk mixture into a serving bowl. Fold in egg whites. Garnish the top with nutmeg. Serve in cups. Serves 6 to 8.

Syllabub

A syllabub, or sillyboo, is a light yet potent frothy drink usually made with heavy cream and wine or fortified wine, but sometimes a liquor. It was once served as a traditional dessert drink for holiday entertaining by Scottish Americans living in the South. Now made in several variations, this recipe includes Scotch whisky.

1 lemon
¼ cup Scotch whisky
¼ cup superfine sugar
1 cup heavy cream

Grate the zest from lemon. Squeeze the juice into a cup or small bowl. Add lemon zest and whisky. Let stand at room temperature, covered, for 4 to 6 hours. Stir in sugar until dissolved. Meanwhile, in a medium bowl, whip cream until soft peaks form. Gradually add the whisky mixture, stirring constantly with a whisk. Spoon into individual stemmed glasses. Refrigerate for about 1 hour before serving. Serves 4.

Het Pint

Once in Scottish towns the celebration of New Year's Eve began with the drinking of Het Pint, *het* meaning hot—a punch made of hot ale, spiced and laced with whisky. It was carried through the streets in copper or toddy kettles shortly before midnight. Noggins of the steaming drink were handed to one and all with a "gude New Year and mony may ye see." Flavored with sugar and frothy with whipped eggs, today it is served very hot in mugs at Scottish-American New Year's holiday celebrations.

1 qt. ale
Freshly grated nutmeg, to taste
¼ cup sugar
2 eggs
½ cup Scotch whisky

In a large saucepan or kettle, heat ale and nutmeg over medium-low heat. Do not boil. Add sugar, leaving to dissolve. Meanwhile, beat eggs in a small bowl. Add ¾ cup of the hot ale mixture. Beat to blend well. Pour into hot ale mixture, stirring. Stir in whisky. Reheat until hot. Beat again. Serve at once in mugs. Serves 4 to 6.

Mint Julep

In Kentucky and other Southern states where Scottish Americans live, one of their favorite beverages has long been the Mint Julep. Few persons agree on the proper way to make the drink. Controversies have persisted for years over whether or not the mint should be crushed, what kind of whisky should be used, and the correct method of serving. Thus, there are innumerable "recipes" for the drink that, of course, is traditional at Kentucky Derby social events but is also good for other occasions. Here is one version from Kentucky. Always serve this ice cold.

1 heaping tsp. confectioners' sugar
2 tsp. water
6 small, tender, fresh mint leaves
2 to 3 oz. Bourbon whiskey

In a chilled silver mug or cup or a tall glass, dissolve sugar in water. Add 4 mint leaves. Bruise leaves gently with a muddler or spoon. Fill the mug, cup, or glass with crushed ice. Stir. Add whiskey. Put in the refrigerator or freezer until well frosted, if desired. Just before serving, add a final splash of whiskey and garnish with 2 mint leaves. Serve at once with or without a small straw. Serves 1.

Rob Roy

This Scottish drink takes its name from the famous Highland outlaw, Rob Roy. It has been a popular drink in America for devotees of Scotch whisky.

2½ oz. Scotch whisky
½ oz. dry vermouth
1 lemon peel

Pour whisky and vermouth into a mixing glass filled with ice. Stir. Strain into a chilled cocktail glass. Twist lemon peel over the drink. Drop peel into the glass. Serves 1.

Scotch Coffee

This is a good after-dinner beverage favored by Scottish Americans.

1 jigger Scotch whisky
Sugar, to taste
1 cup hot brewed coffee
2 tbsp. heavy cream

In a large pottery or heat-resistant glass mug, combine whisky and sugar, allowing sugar to dissolve. Fill the mug with coffee, leaving about ³/₄ inch empty room at the top. Pour cream over the back of a teaspoon to float on top of coffee. Drink coffee through cream. Serves 1.

Toddy

Although there are many variations, a toddy is usually a heated mug of whisky diluted with water and flavored with lemon juice and sugar. It is sipped with slow and loving care as a drink or taken as a cure for colds and as an elixir of life. Originally the beverage was made cold, but over the years the idea of a hot toddy became more convivial. The Scottish poet Robert Burns is said to have enjoyed the drink and was the first to note it in print, in 1786. By then "toddy" was in wide use in America as the name of the hot lemony whisky.

1 lump sugar
Boiling water
2 to 3 oz. Scotch whisky
1 slice lemon or 1 lemon peel

Dissolve sugar in a glass half-full of boiling water with a silver spoon in it to keep the glass from cracking. Add whisky and lemon slice or twist of lemon peel. Stir and sip as hot as possible. Serves 1.

Appljack

Although the early Scottish settlers relished fresh, cooked, or dried apples, a most important product of the fruit was its juice, enjoyed as sweet cider (unfermented) or hard cider (slightly fermented). Due to the bountiful apple orchards, cider was plentiful and inexpensive, enjoyed at all meals and in between.

Whether the distillation process for making hard cider was first perfected in New England or Virginia is not certain, but the drink became popular in both places, known in the former as applejack and the latter as apple brandy. By the late 1600s, almost every prosperous farm had an apple orchard and cider making began almost immediately after the first apples were harvested. Hard cider was the favorite spirit in colonial times. One early book that included directions for making cider described the Scotch Method as one that will have a "bright and pure" liquor.

From the earliest times, New Jersey could claim special honors in our country's apple lore. Plantings there date back to 1632. At one time, hundreds of little distilleries in the state were turning apples into a spirit known as Jersey Lightning. William Laird, a Scot, began producing applejack as early as 1698 in or around Scobeyville, New Jersey in present-day Monmouth County, where his grandson, Robert, founded Laird & Co., the oldest commercial distillery in the United States. According to family lore, William made Scotch whisky back in Scotland and switched to making applejack when he reached the small New Jersey village. It has been said that George Washington was so impressed with the drink that he wrote to the Lairds asking for their recipe.

Laird & Co. is the nation's top producer of apple brandies and the only producer of applejack. It is a splendid drink either straight or in a cocktail.

Jack Rose

Of the various applejack cocktails, the Jack Rose, a flavorful pink-colored beverage, is the best known and best liked, a favorite of many Scottish Americans.

2 oz. applejack
1 tsp. freshly squeezed lemon juice
1 tsp. Grenadine
Ice cubes

Combine all the ingredients in a cocktail shaker. Cover. Shake well. Strain into a chilled cocktail glass. Serves 1.

Governor Spotswood's Champagne Cup

Alexander Spotswood, a Virginia colonial governor of Scottish descent and the person for whom Spotsylvania County is named, is remembered also for mixing business with pleasure during a visit to the Shenandoah Valley in 1716. Upon reaching the crest of the Blue Ridge and casting their eyes upon the Valley, Spotswood and his cavalcade of gentlemen paused to drink several toasts before firing a volley, as they had in their provisions red and white wines, whisky, brandy, rum, champagne, punch, and cider.

At Swift Run Gap near Stanardsville, Virginia, on the Skyline Drive where the Indians guided Spotswood and his merry gentlemen, a marker commemorates the visit. It reads: KNIGHTS OF THE GOLDEN HORSESHOE: NEAR HERE GOVERNOR ALEXANDER SPOTSWOOD AND HIS TROOP OF GENTLEMEN, KNIGHTS OF THE GOLDEN HORSE-SHOE, ON THEIR WAY TO EXPLORE THE LAND BEYOND THE MOUNTAINS, CAMPED ON AUGUST 31, 1716.

One of the governor's favorite drinks was a Champagne cup. Here is an old-time recipe for it.

Spotswood's Champagne Cup/Virginia

Ingredients.—One quart bottle of champagne, two bottles of soda water, one liquor glass of curacoa, two tablespoons of powdered sugar, one pound of pounded ice, a sprig of green borage.

Mode.—Put all the ingredients into a silver cup, regulating the proportion of ice by the state of the weather. Hand the cup around with a clean napkin passed through one of the handles, that the edge of the cup may be wiped after each guest has partaken of the contents thereof.

Arrack Punch

A great colonial beverage called Arrack punch, originally made with a sugarcane-rice liquor then replaced with rum or brandy, has a Scottish connection. For it was one night at a Williamsburg tavern that Peter Jefferson, a young farmer and member of the House of Burgesses, had an extraordinary streak of luck at cards. Before the evening was out he had won a 400-acre tract of land for a single bowl of the tavern's best Arrack punch. Shortly afterward, he wooed and won the hand of Jane Randolph. Their son, Thomas, was born on April 13, 1743.

The drink is now made with lime juice, water, sugar, rum, and a splash of Champagne.

Glasgow Punch

All my Scottish friends from Glasgow, including Mary ("Maisse") Gordon Whitman, are very proud of their city, known for its hospitality and conviviality. Many of their clubs of "jovial festivities" once featured a punch bowl filled with a popular drink made with Caribbean rum, sugar, lime or lemon juice, and spring water. Glasgow Punch is still a traditional drink there and enjoyed by many Scottish Americans.

Here is my favorite recipe for the punch to serve at a party.

1 cup sugar, preferably superfine
7 cups cold water
1 cup fresh lemon juice
¾ cup fresh lime juice
1½ cups light rum

In a large pitcher or punch bowl, stir sugar in 1 cup water, until it is dissolved. Add remaining water, the lemon and lime juices, and rum. Refrigerate until ready to serve. Serve cold. Makes about 2½ qt.

Benjamin Franklin's Orange Shrub

Benjamin Franklin, the distinguished scientist, philosopher, writer, inventor, and statesman, whose grandmother was born in Scotland and came to America as an indentured servant and later married her owner, was very fond of dining and drinking well. Among his numerous papers was a set of recipes and many allusions to food. He also enjoyed his trips to Scotland, where he received an honorary doctorate at the University of St. Andrews in 1759.

His recipe for punch, written in 1737, illustrates that the notable statesman had the talent to write a poetic recipe: "Boy, bring a bowl of China here, Fill it with water cool and clear; Decanter with Jamaica ripe, And spoon of silver, clean and bright, Sugar twice-fin'd in pieces cut, Knife, sive, and glass in order put, Bring forth the fragrant fruit, & then We're happy till the clock strikes ten."

Franklin was also fond of an early American beverage called a shrub, made with a fruit base and brandy or rum. Here is a recipe for one version.

1 qt. light rum
Grated zest of 1 orange
2 cups sugar
2½ qt. orange juice

In a bowl, pour rum over orange zest. Leave 2 to 3 hours. Strain into a bowl, reserving the liquid. Add sugar and orange juice to the liquid, stirring until sugar dissolves. Mix well. Pour into 1 or 2 bottles. Let stand in a cool place for 3 to 4 days before serving. Serves 10 to 12.

Bishop

A popular 18th- and 19th-century drink made with wine, citrus juices, and spices was mentioned by the Scottish writer James Boswell to be a favorite of his traveling companion, Dr. Samuel Johnson. Introduced by Scots to early America, the hot spicy drink, sometimes called a punch, has been traditionally served for holidays. As one saying went, "Fine oranges roasted, with wine in a cup, make a fine Bishop when gentlemen sup."

Here is an old-time recipe.

2 oranges
Several cloves
2 qt. red wine
Small pieces cinnamon
1 piece gingerroot
4 whole allspice
1 cup cognac, slightly heated

Stud oranges with cloves. In a preheated 350-degree oven, bake oranges for about 40 minutes, until cloves begin to turn white and powdery. Meanwhile, heat wine with a cheesecloth bag containing cinnamon, ginger, and allspice. Remove cheesecloth. When oranges are baked, put them in a heatproof punch bowl. Add cognac. Ignite, and as the flames glow, add hot wine. Serve at once. Makes about 2 qt.

Governor Dinwiddie's Sherry Cobbler

Robert Dinwiddie was an energetic Scotsman who was the governor of Virginia from 1751 to 1758 and for whom the state's Dinwiddie County is named. Born near Glasgow, he is known also for "discovering" the military talents of a young man named George Washington.

The cobbler, an American invention, is a cooling sweet beverage, made with wine or liquor, fruit, sugar, and shaved ice, served attractively in a tall glass. It has long been popular with Scottish Americans as a summer drink. Governor Dinwiddie is reported to have been fond of one made with sherry.

Here is a typical recipe for the drink.

1 tsp. confectioners' sugar
2 tsp. water
3 slices orange
Sherry
Ice chips
1 lemon peel

In a tall glass, dissolve sugar in water. Add orange, and fill within ½ inch from the top with sherry. Add ice, and when the glass begins to frost, decorate with a twist of lemon peel. Serve with a straw. Serves 1.

Drambuie

Scotland's oldest and most famous liqueur, Drambuie, pro-nounced *dram-boo-ee,* is a unique spirit made from wild heather honey, special herbs, and the finest malt whiskies. It has a romantic history linked with a very important episode in the country's history, 1746, or "Charlie's Year," as the Highlanders called it, when the Bonnie Prince's Culloden defeat ended his "impossible dream." Official Drambuie lore contends that the prince gave the formula for his personal liqueur to a close friend, Capt. John MacKinnon of the Isle of Skye, as a mark of deep respect and genuine affection. The secret of the drink's preparation has remained with the MacKinnon family, who has marketed the internationally renowned drink as "Prince Charles Edward's Liqueur, A Line With the 45." The name is a translation of the Gaelic phrase *An dram Buidheach,* meaning the drink that satisfies.

Reasonably dry and aromatic in character, the liqueur has an attractive sherry-brown color, showing flecks of gold in the sun "like sunbeams imprisoned on a peat bog."

Drambuie is delicious on its own as an after-dinner cordial, and it makes an excellent base for classic and contemporary cocktails. The liqueur blends perfectly with Scotch whisky in a number of drinks. One of the best is the Rusty Nail, made with 1 oz. Drambuie and 1 oz. Scotch whisky over ice cubes. For an Old Fashioned, combine a twist of lemon peel with 1 oz. Drambuie, shaved ice, and Scotch. Old-time drinks include those named Prince Charlie, Flora Macdonald, Isle of Skye, Robbie Burns, and Mystic Marvel. Scottish Coffee consists of coffee and 1 oz. Drambuie topped with whipped cream, and the liqueur can be added to iced tea.

Hot Buttered Cider

This is a good winter beverage for a small gathering of friends. It is made with sweet apple cider, sold in supermarkets or in the fall at country roadside stands.

About 1 qt. apple cider
4 tsp. sugar
4 dashes freshly grated or ground nutmeg
4 pieces lemon peel
4 sticks cinnamon
4 pats unsalted butter

In a medium saucepan, heat cider over medium-high heat to the boiling point. In each of 4 heat-proof mugs, put 1 tsp. sugar, 1 dash nutmeg, 1 piece lemon peel, and 1 stick cinnamon. Fill the mugs with hot cider, using enough to fill the cups. Top each with 1 pat butter. Stir with cinnamon stick. Serves 4.

Spiced Cider

The annual Christmas Walk in Volcano, Amador County, California, which has taken place since 1982, was inspired by the Alexandria, Virginia, Christmas Walk. At the California event, it is customary to serve complimentary mulled cider.

Here is my favorite recipe for a mulled or spiced cider.

1 qt. apple cider
¼ cup sugar
6 whole cloves
¼-inch piece cinnamon
8 whole allspice
⅛ tsp. salt

In a large saucepan, combine all the ingredients. Bring to a boil. Cool. Let stand overnight. When ready to serve the cider, strain and reheat. Serve hot. Serves 4.

James Monroe's Mint Punch

James Monroe, our fifth president, was born in Westmoreland County, Virginia in 1758 to parents of Scottish descent. He played a sizable role in American history, fighting in the Revolution and holding more offices than any other president: U.S. senator; minister to France, England, and Spain; governor of Virginia; secretary of state and of war; and president from 1817 to 1825.

Monroe's close relationship with Thomas Jefferson brought him to Charlottesville. In 1793 he purchased 1,000 acres adjacent to Monticello and built an estate he called Highland, perhaps because of his Scottish ancestry. Today, on a stunning hilltop at the head of a long lawn studded with ancient trees and surrounded with glorious gardens, stands a modest cream-colored wooden farmhouse known as Ash Lawn-Highland, a 535-acre estate with the atmosphere of a working plantation.

The James Monroe Museum, dedicated to the study, interpretation, and presentation of his life with exhibitions, community events, and educational programs, is located in Fredericksburg, Virginia.

The Historic James Monroe House, 2017 I Street NW, Washington, D.C., is where Secretary of State James Monroe and his wife resided. After Monroe was inaugurated president in March 1817, the house served as his residence until the war-damaged White House was fully restored in September of that year. Today the National Historic Landmark is home to the Arts Club of Washington, where several meetings and social events of The Living Legacy of Scotland are held.

This refreshing mint-flavored punch was enjoyed by President Monroe at Oak Hill, a Virginia plantation where he and his wife, Elizabeth, retired.

⅔ cup sugar
½ cup snipped mint leaves, lightly packed
2 cups hot water
2 cups red grape juice, chilled

2 cups orange juice, chilled
Fresh mint leaves, for garnish

In a medium bowl, combine sugar, snipped mint leaves, and water. Stir until sugar is dissolved. Chill. Strain, discarding mint and reserving liquid. In a pitcher, combine the reserved liquid and grape and orange juices. Serve in a bowl over crushed ice. Garnish with fresh mint leaves. Serves 6.

Tea

"Thank god for tea!" wrote the 19th-century clergyman and writer Sydney Smith. "What would the world do without tea?" Tea has long been a noble beverage that throughout a long and fascinating history has been a healer of man, stimulant of philosophers, inspiration of poets, and symbol of civilization. It's still "the cup that cheers" that Scots around the world treasure. For them it's always teatime.

All tea leaves come from an evergreen tree that originally grew wild in China and Southeast Asia. Traders brought the leaves to Europe, where the delicate aroma and flavor of the brew made with them established tea as a social beverage. By the mid-18th century, taking a cup of tea for refreshment during the day had become a Scottish custom and it was carried to America by early settlers.

Tea quickly became fashionable after it was introduced to the New World, for records show that the Scotswoman in America took great pride in her tea table, teapots, sugar bowl, and silver spoons. She not only brewed several kinds of tea in different pots to please the individual preferences of her guests but created special delicacies to serve with the beverage. There is a collection of Scottish tea wares and drinking vessels at Colonial Williamsburg, Virginia.

Tea varies according to the variety of plant and the region in which it is grown. There are three main types of tea: the most familiar, black; the light and delicate green tea; and the distinctive, partly fermented oolong. A favorite Scottish tea that is called "breakfast tea" was created by a Scot named Drysdale in Edinburgh in 1878 and the firm is still there. Another Scottish name that is synonymous with tea is that of Sir Thomas Lipton, a native of Glasgow who lived briefly in New York.

A Cup of Tea

It is not difficult to make a good cup of tea, but it should be done properly—just before serving. Tea should be made in a good pottery or china pot so it will steep and all the fine flavors and aromas will not escape. Fill the teapot with hot water to heat it before you make the tea. Then empty it, and put in the tea leaves. The usual amount is 1 tsp. leaves per serving cup. Add the water, which must be at a rolling boil when you pour it over the leaves in the pot. Put on the lid and cover with a tea cozy, if desired, to hold in the heat while the tea steeps. Allow 3 to 6 minutes, depending on the variety, for the steeping. Pour and drink. Serve with a choice of milk, sugar, and lemon.

Note: Some people who like very strong tea can include a little more than 1 tsp. per cup. For those who like weak tea, don't cut down on the leaves. Instead, add a little hot water to the tea after you pour it into the cup.

Iced Tea

Brew the tea as above. Allow the tea to cool at room temperature. If refrigerated, it may turn cloudy. Serve preferably with superfine sugar so that it dissolves completely. Or, to make iced tea quickly, pour the brewed strong tea over a glass of ice cubes. It will dilute to the proper strength as the ice melts into it. Serve in tall glasses.

Afternoon Tea

In Scottish-American homes, the custom of inviting friends for a cup of tea is implicit in the word "welcome" and, as a social event, it follows the highest tradition of hospitality. Today many people still find the custom relaxing, entertaining, and a delightful way to get together with friends. Whether a small sociable gathering or a more formal reception, afternoon tea is an event characterized by refinement and taste while still offering gaiety and good cheer.

In choosing foods for a tea, it is customary to serve those that complement the delicacy and lightness of the beverage itself. Dainty sandwiches and breads, small cakes, cookies, and pastries, attractively presented and supplemented by little bowls of candies, nuts, or candied fruits, are good. Scots favor scones, oatcakes, Dundee cake, shortbread, as well as jams and jellies.

Here are suggestions for making tea sandwiches.

Trim crusts from thin-sliced white, whole wheat, or other kinds of bread. Cut into rounds, triangles, diamonds, or squares, if desired. Have them open or closed. Spread or fill with any of the following fillings. Plan 3 to 4 sandwiches per person.

Fillings

1. Sliced, peeled cucumbers topped with mayonnaise and garnished with fresh dill
2. Chopped fresh watercress mixed with softened butter and grated onion
3. Minced cooked chicken mixed with almonds and sour cream
4. Strawberry jam mixed with chopped walnuts and cream cheese
5. Cream cheese mixed with chopped green pepper and onion and Worcestershire sauce

High Tea

In America, it is a common mistake to call an elaborate or "high-class" tea a high tea, which actually is not grand or formal. "Too old to be lunch, too young to be dinner," it's an informal evening meal, a practical and substantial supper served as everyone comes home from work or school. It generally centers around some hearty meat or fish dish, or perhaps kippers, sausages, and eggs. For centuries in Scotland it's been a happy family gathering at the end of the working day.

As one Scottish friend explained, "It's a meal to be proud of and to enjoy with our cups of tea and such homemade treats as jam, breads, scones, bannocks, pancakes, fruit loaf, and especially cakes."

Index